MOSCOW SUMMER

Moscow Summer

BY MIHAJLO MIHAJLOV

Foreword by Myron Kolatch

Introduction, Notes and Biographical Information
by Andrew Field

FARRAR, STRAUS AND GIROUX | NEW YORK
A New Leader Book

CONTENTS

Foreword by Myron Kolatch   vii

Introduction by Andrew Field   3

Part I

Moscow   11
Yugoslavia   16
MGU   18
The Literary Situation   20
Academician Nikolai Gudzy   35
Mikhailovsky in Uzkoe   36
The Search for Golosovker   38
Vladimir Dudintsev   41
Tamara Zhirmunskaya   47
Films   49

Theaters   52
Leonid Leonov   62

Part II

Concentration Camp Themes   66
Labor Camp Folklore   76
Bella Akhmadulina   85
Bondaryov   88
Vladimir Tendryakov   93
Viktor Shklovsky   98
Bulat Okudzhava   104
The Apologist of Abstractionism   114
Evgeny Vinokurov   116
Ilya Ehrenburg   119
Lakshin and Solzhenitsyn   126

Part III

Voznesensky   129
Zagorsk   134
Russian Philosophy   137
Anti-Semitism   140
The Psychology of Homo Sovieticus   145
Conclusions and Perspectives   163
Biographical Information   171
Mihajlov's Open Letter   209
Index of Names   217

FOREWORD

Rarely does the reading public get the chance to glimpse how a particular magazine does what it does, or why (and often the public has good cause to wonder whether there is really any conscious process involved at all). In the case of *The New Leader,* it is probably fair to say that one feature which has made it at least an occasional topic of conversation has been its publication of such things as Viktor Nekrasov's "Travel Notes in America," the transcript of "The Trial of Iosif Brodsky," "Poems by Aleksandr Solzhenitsyn," Abram Tertz's "Thought Unaware," and Mihajlo Mihajlov's *Moscow Summer.* The last also being the first of what is envisioned as a wide-ranging series of new books to be issued jointly by Farrar, Straus and Giroux and *The New Leader,* this seems a proper place to detail the events leading to its appearance.

In January 1965 the Belgrade literary magazine *Delo* published the initial installment of *Moscow Summer*. In February the next installment appeared. Since *Delo* is about as widely read in Yugoslavia as the *Prairie Schooner* is in the United States, neither segment raised the smallest ripple of excitement at home or abroad. Not until the end of the first week of February anyway.

On February 6, an anonymous Belgrade dispatch in the New York *Times* reported that a young Yugoslav scholar named Mihajlo Mihajlov had "stirred the ire of the Soviet Embassy" with his account of a summer visit to the USSR in a magazine called *Delo*. The account occupied a total of 70-odd pages over two issues. The cause of consternation, however, was the author's observation that "The first 'death camps' were not founded by the Germans, but by the Soviets. In 1921, near Arkhangelsk, they set up Kolmogor camp, for the sole purpose of physically destroying the prisoners. It operated successfully for many years. . . . Even in the matter of genocide Hitler had been anticipated. On the eve of World War II numerous peoples in the regions along the Turkish-Iranian border were deported to Northern Siberia where, unaccustomed to the cold climate, they died like flies. . . ."

Coming from a comradely Communist country, the indictment was certainly startling (although not without precedent, if one recalls what was being written in Yugoslavia immediately following the Tito-Stalin split). Our own curiosity, though, centered on what else those 70 pages had to say, and it was heightened on February 11 by the news that an injunction had been granted stopping the sale of *Delo*. We began casting around for copies of the January and the banned February numbers. But the search did not take on urgency until March 4, when *Kommunist*, the official Party weekly, suddenly published an attack against Mihajlov that Marshal Tito had delivered three weeks earlier (on February 11, too), while speaking privately to a delegation of public prosecutors:

> You see what happened with that article in *Delo?* The public prosecutor ought to have banned it straight away, and made the decision public. . . . You ought to have instituted proceedings immediately against the person who wrote that article, and published your decision in the press. It was necessary to know that an indictment had been raised against him, that he was a reactionary who slandered a great event—the October Revolution. . . .
>
> It is really strange that such things happen to us when we have organs of management both in the collectives of newspaper boards and in printing offices. . . .
>
> Likewise, we must not permit instances of anyone in our Socialist country defending Hitler's concentration camps, where living men were burned to death, where millions and tens of millions of people, children and old men alike, were destroyed. . . .
>
> There have been other examples of the same kind. In such matters you must take action immediately and energetically. . . .
>
> It seems to me that this tendency, which we used

to call Djilasism, is now assuming a new form. As I have said, this is being propagated particularly in the press, and this is very dangerous.

For *The New Leader*, the reference to Djilas had special significance:

Nine years earlier, with the sound of Soviet tanks and troops echoing through the streets of Budapest as they brutally mopped up the Hungarian Freedom Fighters, and with festering discontent in Warsaw threatening to break out into a pitched battle against the regime, two of the magazine's editors wondered who in the Communist world might be sufficiently repelled by the ugly turn of events to raise his voice in a meaningful appraisal. While various names were being discarded, a friend dropped in and suggested Milovan Djilas. The volcanic Montenegrin, once an ardent admirer of Stalin, had recently been dropped as Vice President of Yugoslavia and heir apparent to Marshal Tito because of his open expression of "heretical" views. The idea was intriguing. A brief cable was sent off requesting an article analyzing the developments in Hungary and Poland. Not knowing Djilas' precise address, we simply addressed it "Belgrade."

Four days later Milovan Djilas' historic article, "The Storm in Eastern Europe" (*New Leader*, November 19, 1956), arrived by regular air mail. Less than 24 hours after it was on the stands, the New York office of International News Service called. The INS correspondent in Vienna, a personal friend of Mrs. Djilas, had just spoken to her by phone and learned that the secret police had come to search Djilas' apartment and arrest him. When Mrs. Djilas asked why they were taking away her husband, they cited his article in *The New Leader*.

Repeated requests to Marshal Tito that the magazine be permitted to supply Djilas with counsel at his subsequently announced trial, or else be allowed to have a legal observer present, went unanswered. In secret session, Djilas received a three-year sentence and was sent off to Sremska Mitrovica, where he had previously been imprisoned for his activities as a Bolshevik. Shortly afterward, publication of *The New Class* (already out of his hands at the time of his arrest), resulted in his being given an additional seven-year sentence. In 1961, Tito decided to release his old friend—who was suffering from a severe rheumatic condition—on probation. Not one to be cowed, Djilas soon wrote a short story, "The War" (*New Leader*, April 16, 1962), then another book that incurred official wrath, *Conversations with Stalin*. He was returned to Sremska Mitrovica to serve a nine-year term.

Thus Tito's linking Mihajlov with Djilas intensified our search. However, during the strange three-week gap between the time the Marshal delivered his remarks and the time they were made public, a series of other developments had kept our interest in *Moscow Summer* alive.

On February 27, Soviet Ambassador Aleksandr Mikhailovich Puzanov delivered a sharply worded note to President Tito. A Communist diplomat who claimed to have read it called it "a veritable cannonade," in which the Kremlin declared it "had reason to believe" *Moscow Summer's* publication was not unintentional. February 28, the Yugoslav weekly *Nin* appeared carrying a long, vitriolic editorial entitled "Mihajlo Mihajlov's Strange Summer," charging the young writer was a "Right-wing agent of White Russian and anti-Communist circles." March 1, Mihajlov responded in a lengthy open letter to *Nin's* editor, Risto Tosovic. (He sent it to 290 Yugoslav newspapers because of *Nin's* failure to run a previous letter of his, but it did not get into print. See appendix for full text.) Mihajlov protested:

When the Civil War and the intervention ended in Russia, and when my parents arrived in Yugoslavia, my father was seventeen years of age and my mother seven. My father studied and graduated at a *Yugoslav* university, did his military service in the *Yugoslav* Army, took an active part in the *Yugoslav* national liberation struggle, and for years directed the *Yugoslav* Scientific Institute.

I was born [September 26, 1934] in the *Yugoslav* town of Pancevo, attended primary school in the *Yugoslav* town of Zrenjanin, completed my secondary education in the *Yugoslav* town of Sarajevo, attended and graduated from universities in the *Yugoslav* cities of Belgrade and Zagreb, constructed a *Yugoslav* highway in the ranks of the youth work brigades, served a term in the *Yugoslav* Army, was elected instructor at a *Yugoslav* university, and in my documents, under the heading "Nationality," the word "Yugoslav" is written. . . .

You are probably well aware that I was not in the

Soviet Union as a "tourist," as you repeatedly state. I spent a whole month in the USSR in 1964 under the Cultural Exchange Program between the USSR and the Socialist Federal Republic of Yugoslavia. A Soviet university instructor made a return visit of one month to Yugoslavia. I was nc one's "guest," and had no need to lie about what I saw in gratitude for the hospitality shown me!

What can one do? I feel more respect for the Russian people than for the Soviet authorities. I did not abuse anybody's confidence. I did not write a single word about my conversations with distinguished Russian authors without receiving their permission for this in advance whenever it was a case of conversations without witnesses. . . .

On March 2, Mihajlov was interviewed in Zadar, the Adriatic coastal city where he was a lecturer in Slavic Languages and Literatures, Faculty of Philosophy, at a branch of Zagreb University. According to David Binder, the knowledgeable and conscientious *Times* correspondent, he expressed astonishment at the furor he had aroused: "I have been writing for years about Soviet literature, and I certainly did not consider *Moscow Summer* the strongest or most important thing I had written. It was merely reportage."

In fact, the young Dostoevsky scholar, who has developed a strong interest in post-Stalin literature as well, had lectured frequently on the Yugoslav radio and contributed to a dozen leading papers and reviews in Zagreb,

Novi Sad and Belgrade. Moreover, an article of his in the June 1964 *Forum*, organ of the Yugoslav Academy of Sciences and Arts, comparing "Dostoevsky's *House of the Dead* and Solzhenitsyn," discusses death camps in greater detail than *Moscow Summer*, citing both Soviet and International Red Cross sources. Yet it stimulated no repercussions, no political recriminations, from Moscow or Belgrade.

Similarly, before going to Russia in July Mihajlov wrote a three-part essay for the Serbian monthly *Kolo*, the third part of which was suppressed because of its contention that "Even Christianity, as a religion of freedom, can become the basis for a just organization of society on earth, and not the so-called 'national laws of development' on which the theory of 'scientific' Socialism is based. . . ." In the winter *Kolo's* editor, Sasha Veres, was dismissed for using the first two parts, but in July no step was taken to prevent Mihajlov's participation in the Soviet-Yugoslav Cultural Exchange Program.

Mihajlov had completed *Moscow Summer* in October 1964 and submitted it to *Letopis Matica Srpska* in Novi Sad. The editors returned it with a note explaining that recent articles on Poland and Hungary, having "similar themes," had caused them "enough troubles." The manuscript was then sent to *Forum*, where it was held for two months and such things as the concentration camp songs were edited out. Meanwhile, Mihajlov had mailed another copy to *Delo*, whose co-editor, Milosav Mirkovic, accepted it. (Mirkovic, also dismissed and scheduled to stand trial, was allowed to return to his post after giving the prosecutors a statement that Mihajlov would not permit any editorial changes—which Mihajlov emphatically denied.)

Asked at his March 2 Zadar interview whether he thought he would be arrested, Mihajlov answered: "Maybe, but this is not like the Soviet Union." Two days later, the Tito statement was released and Mihajlov was jailed.

Our hope now was that *Delo* had been mailed out to subscribers before being confiscated; that we could find someone who had received it either in this country or on the Continent. The day the injunction stopping its sale was issued, over 1,000 copies of the magazine were seized. Efforts by Western journalists to learn the total print run met with the response that this was "a secret," but it was estimated to be around 1,500. Within a week our hope materialized. We located both the January and February *Delo* in Cambridge, Massachusetts.

Once in hand, it immediately became apparent that our curiosity had been justified. For while Mihajlov had indeed written revealingly of the Soviet concentration camps and their legacy—as the news stories kept stressing—that constituted only a very small portion of his essay, perhaps ten percent. What made *Moscow Summer* remarkable was the unique *tour d'horizon* it offered of the current Soviet literary and cultural scene. Recording notes of conversations with the young and the old, the famous and the less well known, it not only contained a wealth of new information but presented a view of Soviet literary life rarely seen in the West. In an expanded number dated March 29, *The New Leader* published *Moscow Summer* in full—or, to be more precise, we thought we had published it in full until Mihajlov's trial.

The trial took place in the Zadar District Court on April 29. Mihajlov, after spending 37 days in jail, had been released April 10 to prepare his case. He was indicted under Article 175 of the Yugoslav Criminal Code for "damaging the reputation of a foreign state," and under Article 125 of the Press Law for mailing his manuscript to a Rome publisher after *Delo* was banned. Originally only suspended from his teaching post, he was expelled from the Philosophical Faculty April 28. A student had written across the door of his office: "Long live Mihajlov, long live freedom."

The morning of the trial, colleagues and students filled most of the 110 seats and all of the standing space in the courtroom. Present, too, was Anatole Shub, Central European correspondent for the Washington *Post* and former managing editor of *The New Leader*. His excellent analysis of the Mihajlov affair in the June issue of the British magazine *Encounter* included a vivid description of the proceedings.

The five-hour hearing was conducted before two silent "people's" judges and one professional jurist, presiding judge Branko Novakovic, who did the questioning. In his opening statement, the prosecutor cited what Mihajlov had written about Soviet concentration camps, accusing him of having "abused the freedom of expression which exists in our country." Mihajlov was the only witness.

Short, stocky, clean-cut and soft-spoken, his testimony was nevertheless uncompromising.

"I have presented historical facts, and I was aware that by presenting such facts this would not be agreeable to the party concerned." But, Mihajlov insisted, his intention was not to offend the USSR. He had presented "historical facts" on Soviet camps in an effort to provide a better understanding of the growing volume of Soviet literature on the subject. And throughout the five-hour session both he and his attorney, Dr. Ivo Glowatzky (who said he was defending Mihajlov "as a matter of professional conscience"), pointed to truth and "historical fact."

Why then, the court wanted to know, did Mihajlov collate Soviet camps with Nazi death camps? "This was not a coincidence. I consider that Stalinism is no better than Fascism. This is why I have made the comparison, to show that totalitarianism is always the same regardless of whether it is Fascist or Stalinist, no matter under what sign and no matter what social system it tends to realize."

Mihajlov added that he thought the situation was improving in the Soviet Union. Asked to elaborate, he said he discussed this in a third part of his essay that had not been published. Turning to the second count of his indictment, Mihajlov maintained that he did not know *Delo* had been permanently banned when he responded to an Italian publisher's request for material for a possible book, that in any event he sent him the *Forum*-edited manuscript and the unpublished third section, and that he had made no publication commitment.

The next morning the courtroom was again packed,

awaiting the verdict. Mihajlov was found guilty on both counts, receiving a sentence of five months on each that was combined into one nine-month term, less the 37 days already served. Apparently the judges had decided that truth was irrelevant, and had rejected the logic of his argument against the second charge. Not surprisingly, Dr. Glowatzky announced he would appeal the decision, labeling it "harsh." Nor was it surprising that most of the spectators agreed, describing the sentence as "politically motivated" and saying it had been a "political trial." But the references in news stories to a "third part" were a surprise. (We did not yet have the full text of Mihajlov's open letter, which also mentions "the third part of my travel notes.") Obviously we had not published *Moscow Summer* in full after all.

Eager to complete what we had started, we began contacting writers and readers of *The New Leader* who might have some clue to the missing section. If it was out of Yugoslavia, it surely would turn up somewhere. For two weeks we were wholly unsuccessful; many of the people we contacted were not aware another part existed until we told them about it.

We had pretty much given up when a call came from a long-time contributor and close friend at Stanford University, in California, whom we had not contacted: "Listen, do you know there is another part to the Mihajlov? . . . Well, a colleague of mine here has a mimeographed French translation of it." Since we frown upon translations from translations—it is difficult enough to do a faithful rendering of an original—we asked our friend to inquire about the source of the French version. It had come from a man we did not know personally, but we thought a friend in London could help. A trans-Atlantic call confirmed our suspicion, the man in London called the man in Paris, and that night the original text of the missing third part—much different and more controversial than the first two parts, about which all the fuss had been made—was on its way to us. "Moscow Summer—Part III" was published for the first time in *The New Leader* of June 7.

On June 23, with Marshal Tito away visiting the Soviet Union, the Supreme Court of Croatia decided Mihajlov did not have to go to jail. Hearing his appeal in Zagreb, it dismissed the first charge against him on the grounds that he may have offended the "feelings" of the Soviet Union, but his work did not contain "elements of a criminal offense." Upholding the charge that he had distributed banned material in violation of the Press Law, the court suspended the five-month sentence and placed Mihajlov on probation for two years.

On the surface, everything seems to have come to a happy ending for all concerned. And *Moscow Summer* is achieving the permanence it deserves—despite some unevenness and occasional traces of naïveté—by being published as a book. In the strange, unpredictable world of power politics, though, happy endings have never been the vogue. Mihajlov, expelled from his teaching job as "morally undesirable," has been refused readmittance to the Zadar faculty; his views, it was stated, are "contrary to the present life, attitude and social system" of Yugoslavia. In addition, at this writing, he has been refused a visa to accept invitations to visit Columbia University and the University of California in Berkeley. Perhaps his royalties from this book, being held in escrow, will eventually help alleviate his economic difficulties.

In any event, important questions remain to be answered: Why did the Soviet leaders become so exercised over what one would have expected them to accept in the post-"cult" era? Why did Marshal Tito elect to catapult Mihajlov to prominence by singling out his work for censure? Was it really because of Kremlin pressure alone? Or was it because most of Mihajlov's criticisms of Soviet society apply equally to Yugoslav society? Does Tito's attack reflect, as some have suggested, a renascence of the cult of personality in Belgrade? Or does it, as others have implied, merely represent an act "for the benefit" of Moscow?

The questions could go on and on. The answers will vary with the specialist. Only one thing can be said with certainty: For the Mihajlovs of the world the proper ending is still to be written.

August 1965   Myron Kolatch

MOSCOW SUMMER

INTRODUCTION

> "Oh, impious Squire! Oh Nourishment and Favours ill bestow'd! Is this my Reward for having got thee a Government. . . ."
>
> *Don Quixote*

There is a delightful story, perhaps apocryphal, which says that Mihajlov's father, a former White Russian officer who settled in Yugoslavia, used to chase the tax collector down the main street of Zadar with saber drawn, and this might account for the portion of "Russian quixoticism" in his son's scholarly and intellectual nature. But the "quixotic" element of what Mihajlov has written, fascinating and important as it is, belongs to the political sphere and is, I think, secondary and extrinsic to the real significance of *Moscow Summer*. For while *Moscow Summer* is peppered with explosive and controversial passages, the substance of Mihajlov's essay is concerned primarily not with Soviet politics, but rather, with Rus-

3

sian culture. As a Yugoslav, Mihajlov was in a position to meet many more Soviet writers than a Westerner could have in so short a time (though if his guide had not received official permission, Mihajlov would not have been able to see many of the people he met), and being himself of Russian origin, he was able to appreciate and utilize what he saw to the fullest degree.

Moscow Summer contains a broad survey of contemporary Soviet poetry and prose (conversations with and commentaries on over twenty writers); judgment of the current state of Soviet literary scholarship with discussion of specific books; remarks—again, both general and specific—on Soviet theater, cinema, and art; a survey of twentieth century Russian philosophy; commentary on Soviet songs and "folklore" (concentration camp songs), not only written about, but also written down; an account of Soviet student life; and much, much more. The irony of it all is that the Yugoslavs themselves, with their traditional East European disdain for everything Russian, could not be much stirred by such a chronicle, no matter how excellent, and when *Moscow Summer* first appeared there was actually very little commotion.

Americans and West Europeans, however, have no reason for such studied indifference, and, in fact, have a deep interest in Russia, even if it is only the interest that is inevitable in one's "rival." It is for this reason that perhaps the most important service of Mihajlov's essay—and it is one he could hardly have been aware of—is the fresh light which it throws on our conception of Russia. The Soviet Union has served and serves a particular need for the Western intellectual, and too often his Russia corresponds more closely to his own inner wants than to any more objective reality. "As long as the outrages in our South continue," one of America's best-known poets wrote me not too long ago, "I feel that we have no right to protest anything that happens in the Soviet Union"; and, at the other extreme, an equally eminent English novelist has written: "Our literary freedom in the West is really an allelomorph of apathy. Better to throw your work at the lions than into a great silence." Both statements represent honest introspection, but note how the formulation is made. Well, everyone has his own Russia, I suppose, and it is not my purpose here to champion any one of them, but merely to point out how Russia frequently becomes an abstract alternative or emotional point of reference.

Mihajlov's essay complicates those Russias. In *Moscow Summer* there are no ecstatic descriptions of poetry readings before "utterly mesmerized young Russians." It is not that the poetry readings are not held, not that many Soviet poets have not written *engagé* verse—it is, rather, that such poetry readings are no more representative of what is really happening in contemporary Russian poetry than, say, a reading in a Greenwich Village coffee house would be of American poetry, and that, while we may welcome Evgeny Evtushenko's political involvement, we should remember that Robert Lowell (and, God knows, Evtushenko is no Lowell) sent a letter instead of writing a poem. Mihajlov himself is strongly committed—his arrest is ample testimony to that—but he evidently feels that anti-Semitism and bureaucratic despotism are too serious to deal with in histrionic flourishes; and he knows that the best Russian poets today are following Robert Lowell's example, not Evtushenko's, writing serious poetry and taking their stands as citizens (and in a way, I might add, that is often far more carefully considered and effective than the stand taken by Lowell) without confusing the two duties. Mihajlov does not even discuss Evtushenko—there is one slighting reference to him and a comment on his falling popularity—but he does discuss Novella Matveeva, Evgeny Vinokurov, Bella Akhmadulina, Andrei Voznesensky, Leonid Martynov, Tamara Zhirmunskaya—all poets who have heretofore been rarely presented to the Western reader (except perhaps Voznesensky, who is usually spoken of as a "better Evtushenko") but who show much greater promise to win a place in the history of Russian literature. Other portions of *Moscow Summer* likely to surprise many Western readers include a cold, hard look at Ilya Ehrenburg, Mikhail Sholokhov, and Leonid Leonov, and high praise for and an extensive discussion of Evgeny Shvarts and Bulat Okudzhava, two major figures in modern Soviet literature usually accorded only a breezy sentence or two in surveys.

In the third and concluding section of *Moscow Summer* there is a significant change of approach and tone. Here Mihajlov, instead of concentrating on individuals, comes directly to grips with the many broad and complicated problems and questions concerning the Soviet Union which were implicit in his preceding remarks. This portion of *Moscow Summer* will doubtless annoy some readers who will consider it too general and lacking verisimilitude, while it will strike others as being very much to the point and by far the best portion of the essay. To treat a subject as elusive, controversial, and important as "the psychology of Homo Sovieticus" is an act of courage, especially in a foreigner. The portrait he draws is unpleasant, but by and large all too accurate. We have only to recall Konstantin Paustovsky's famous 1956 "Drozdov speech" (the reference is to a character in Dudintsev's novel *Not By Bread Alone*) in which Paustovsky scathingly refers to the "stinking well-being of these Drozdovs" which has been built at the cost of the lives of countless innocent Russians. The problem of Homo Sovieticus, as Mihajlov takes care to point out, is in essence a psychological and moral one, and a problem of frightening scope since it involves close to ten million people, the ones, moreover, who are the real determinants of the fate of the Soviet Union.

Mihajlov details not only the outward characteristics of the Homo Sovieticus (". . . a more or less constabulary character . . . strongly plebeian . . . easy to recognize after a few words. . . ."), but also the underlying roots of his "disbelief in man (and all mistrust of others reflects a lack of confidence in oneself), and the conviction that, without paternal care and leadership, he will fail." Mihajlov would have Yugoslavia hold up to the Soviet Union the way out of this morass, and this is made clear when he scornfully writes: "It is completely unimaginable to Homo Sovieticus, it is absurd and incredible that someone somewhere in the world could print his own opinions in the newspapers, opinions which do not coincide with those of the 'official program' of the community he lives in."

It can be fairly said that the sum of his own evidence in no way justifies Mihajlov's optimistic outlook for the Soviet future at the conclusion of his essay. (Moreover, the banning of *Moscow Summer* makes even Mihajlov's confidence in the Yugoslav model seem somewhat premature, although it must be granted that an essay like *Moscow Summer* could never have reached the printing press in present-day Poland, and probably not in Hungary, either.) Mihajlov suggests the Chinese threat as one factor which will serve to move the Soviet Union closer to the West, but, since the Homo Sovieticus lived through the onslaught of Hitler's Germany without undergoing any lasting change in character, it is doubtful that the so-called "Yellow Peril" will bring about *that* end. The problem is serious, as I myself can testify on the basis of several frank conversations with Soviet intellectuals in which I was each time surprised by the pessimism of their forecasts for the establishment of some sort of democratic tolerance within the framework of Communism—no guess was this side of forty years! Thus the optimism expressed by Mihajlov may finally prove illusory, but we can accept it at its face value since it is made in full cognizance of the actual state of things; it is perhaps the hope of a new generation—Mihajlov is just thirty-one years old—a generation which is searching for fresh, yet hard-nosed solutions to old problems.

The primary virtues of *Moscow Summer*, it seems to me, are its youthful sensitivity and alertness (the essay contains some of the freshest and most revealing Soviet literary gossip we have had in years), and also—indeed, perhaps most of all—its supple responses to divergent phenomena. Mihajlov knows how and when to be cold, enthusiastic, scholarly, or intensely personal. Any one pattern of response or interest would be unequal to the subject. *Moscow Summer* is not without its faults, both of omission and commission. The fall of Khrushchev has revealed many of Mihajlov's political judgments to be unfounded, and some of his literary pronouncements may be questioned, too. But taken in its entirety, the picture is remarkably inclusive and "true." I think that everyone who writes on Russia would want to make certain changes of emphasis and content in *Moscow Summer*, but the fact remains that it was Mihajlov who had the intellectual grasp and dexterity to capture the most vital portion of the contemporary Soviet experience in a single coherent unit. In a very real sense, this is the book we all ought to have written but—somehow—didn't. And just as *Moscow Summer* causes the large majority of previous Western accounts of Russian intellectual life to seem inadequate if not downright silly now, it may well be that the greatest value of *Moscow Summer* will be its influence on future Western reportage of Russian literature and Soviet politics, thereby effecting a significant step forward in our understanding of the Soviet Union and the enormously important changes, both cultural and political, which are taking place there.

July 1965   Andrew Field

Part I

MOSCOW

To begin with, nothing in Moscow is as one expects or imagines it to be from reading the Soviet or even the Western press:

Walking along the streets, one is struck by the many large tanks for dispensing *kvas,* the national drink.

At every step there are also soda dispensers. One kopek buys a cup of plain soda water; for three kopeks raspberry juice is included.

The walls of the houses are covered with posters: The crooner Emil Horowitz is in town.

In each district there is a *vytrezvitel',* a dispensary for sobering up drunks. Champagne is sold by the glass, and one can drink it standing at the bar. A liter of vodka costs as much as six long-playing records, and I cannot understand where all the drunks come from, yet at night you often meet drunks. During the day, sober people approach you asking for a cigaret. This seems to be an accepted custom; cigarets are not expensive. They are generally of poor quality, though, and when the Bulgarian *Solntse* cigarets reach the tobacco shops people form queues and stock up.

In the outlying sections of town, it is dangerous to go into the streets at night despite numerous patrols of *druzhinniki*, the special people's militia.

The subway system is remarkable. Every minute or so a train arrives, and everything works with precision. On every corner there are information booths. For two kopeks you can get the number of the bus, trolley, or subway that will take you where you want to go.

Moscow is really enormous. Today it ranks among the five biggest cities in the world—with New York, London, Tokyo and Shanghai. The people are uncommonly rude to one another. In a restaurant you take a seat at an empty table and immediately the waiter comes yelling, "Don't you see the one *there* is not filled up yet? What's the matter with you, are you blind?" The same thing happens in the shops, on buses, and on street cars. Foreigners, however, are not subjected to such treatment. For example, although I had an official reservation at the hotel on the Kotlyarskaya Quay, which I chose because of its central location, the clerk at first refused even to discuss the matter with me. "I am telling you, we have no vacant rooms, so why are you standing here?" she said. When I showed her my passport, she apologized: "Pardon me, I thought you were a Russian." And she found me a room.

Do Muscovites read much? Every day, riding on the Metro for an hour or more, I counted the people with books in their hands. Out of 20 to 30 passengers in a car, three or four were reading books. Hardly anybody reads newspapers. This is understandable because the Soviet papers are still dull. It seems probable that the same percentage would read books in any other country if their newspapers were as uninteresting and the subway journeys as long. The only paper you do see people reading is *Vechernaya Moskva* (*Moscow Evening News*) which contains film and theater listings, divorce announcements, criticism, etc.

The Lenin Metro, the Lenin Moscow State University, the Lenin Central Library, and even the Lenin Moscow Circus! It is strange how these people do not notice that if something is repeated too often, it loses all significance.

In restaurants, shops, buses, museums, railway stations and airports—everywhere, everywhere there are red billboards with two kinds of signs. One, "Here works the Brigade of Communist Labor," the other, "Here works the Brigade fighting for the title of the Brigade of Communist Labor."

One afternoon in Gorky Street, in the very center of Moscow, I observed women standing in a queue. It turned out that ladies' umbrellas were on sale. Generally speaking, electric appliances and cameras are extremely cheap, while textiles, shoes and vodka are incredibly expensive.

Moving about the city, one frequently sees "homeopathic" pharmacies.

And in front of the Lenin Mausoleum on Red Square, there are always long queues. They are artificially created, however, since the Mausoleum is open only from 11 A.M. to 2 P.M., and not every day at that. With six million inhabitants in Moscow and innumerable groups visiting from the provinces, it is no wonder such a long line forms during these few hours. Inside, one experiences a strange —one might say mystical—sensation seeing Lenin lying under glass. You can see stubble on his unshaven cheeks. There is solemn silence. Still, one is not certain—is he made of wax? Probably not, for he would look more natural if he were made of wax. In the Mausoleum soldiers stand on every second step, carefully watching the hands of visitors and following every movement they make. You are not allowed to carry anything with you.

At the Tretyakov Gallery, in the room with Socialist Realist paintings, the Gallery attendant told me: "You know, I don't even look at the things here, but I spend whole nights in the vaults—you should see the beauty there! You are young, you will still see those paintings exhibited here." We were interrupted, so I could not find out what paintings she had in mind.

The newspapers were attacking a young painter, Ilya Glazunov, who was having an exhibition in Moscow. I tried to visit the exhibition. It was impossible; the queue was as long as the one in front of the Mausoleum. Other exhibitions were deserted—and rightly.

Half of Russia's history rests in the cemetery of the Novodevichi Monastery. At the mystic poet Vladimir Solovyov's grave, somebody has been taking care of the flowers.

There are 40 churches active in Moscow today. They are so overcrowded that it is difficult to get in. Most of the churchgoers are elderly men and women, but there are girls as well. The "Parks of Culture and Recreation" are special attractions, especially Gorky Central Park. These are huge green complexes full of all kinds of amusements, something like the Vienna Prater. Numerous open-air theaters offer free daily vocal, instrumental and folk music concerts by various amateur companies, and by well-known professionals. Merry-go-rounds spin, dance orchestras play melodies popular 15 years ago (I was amused by *Tico-Tico* and *Domino*), and the girls dance with one another. Generally speaking, one can see everywhere that there are many more women than men in the Soviet Union. Now the number of women is more than 20 per cent greater than the number of men, and the gap is constantly increasing. In addition, many young men are in the Army or away at various Siberian construction sites.

Very often in the evening there are fireworks in Gorky Park. Bread and circuses! However, the wealthier Muscovites amuse themselves differently. Most people in "higher circles" spend the summer in small suburban forest villages, in wooden houses known as *dachas*. They commute back and forth to work every day.

YUGOSLAVIA

"You, in Yugoslavia, are certainly in the avant-garde," one of the most famous Soviet writers told me—and so did many other Soviet people, in almost the same words, each time I recalled the section of Dostoevsky's *Diary* where, quite gratuitously, he suddenly prophesies that in 100 years the South Slavs will be the ones who will perform a major service for Russia.

On the whole, Yugoslavia is much more present in Russia than Russia is in Yugoslavia. Wherever I went I heard the hit song from our picture *Love and Fashion* sung in translation, and occasionally in the original. Posters announced the production by the touring Ljubljana Opera of *Tribe from the Other World*, concerts by Radmila Karaklajic, and football matches between Yugoslav and Soviet teams. At the cinema you could watch *Love and Fashion* and other Yugoslav films; in the display window of the Tass News Agency only photographs from Yugoslavia were exhibited; on newspaper stands a small collection of Yugoslav contemporary humor was on sale. On television I saw the young and talented Yugoslav pianist, Bozena Griner.

In Leningrad, I was told it was impossible to lay hands on a copy of a Yugoslav weekly, *Arena*—the minute it arrives at the newsstands it is sold out. Bookshop windows feature two thick volumes of *The History of Yugoslavia* (published by the Academy of Science of the USSR, 1963). In the Dostoevsky Museum, the book *Dostoevsky among the Serbs* by Milisav Babovic is exhibited in a prominent place. M. S. Balakin, Professor of Yugoslav Literature at Moscow University, will soon publish a *Collection of Yugoslav Popular Proverbs* which he edited together with Radmila Djordjevic-Grigorijev. In short—a real cult of Yugoslavia.

But my greatest pleasure was to hear a young University teacher say: "You, in Yugoslavia, you are doing an enormous service by publishing Boris Pil'nyak, Evgeny Zamyatin, Lev Shestov and other modernists. You see, now we are following you. Aside from the Yugoslavs, such service is rendered only by the Italian Communists." He explained: "The Italians have published Pasternak and the famous book on Dostoevsky by M. M. Bakhtin, and Bukharin's works are being printed."

It is an interesting and symptomatic fact that the Soviets rehabilitate an authentic Russian creative artist only after he has been recognized by Western Communist parties.

Unfortunately, Yugoslav literature is little known apart from the works of Nusic, Dobrica Cosić, Branko Ćopić, Desanka Maksimović and Ivo Andrić.[1] Except for experts, nobody ever heard of Krleža. And right now in the Soviet Union they would certainly benefit by reading *The Dialectic Antibarbarus, Preface to Transdravian Motifs* and many other works of Krleža.

[1] Works by Ćopić, Krleža, and Andrić are available in the recently published anthology, *Death of a Simple Giant and Other Modern Yugoslav Stories* (Vanguard, 1965).

MGU

Moskovsky Gosudarstvenny Universitet: The Moscow State University of Lomonosov. The grandiose building on Lenin's Hills. There are no hills, however; the site is only slightly higher than the central part of Moscow. The University is a worthy monument of the "cult" era. A nonfunctional mammoth colossus with a sharp point 100 feet tall topped by a giant star. It has a tower on each corner and high up on the towers there are statues. It is in the same style as the "Home of Culture" in Warsaw. The basic feeling the University building inspires is that of helplessness and of one's own insignificance. I have seen bigger skyscrapers in Italy, but they had no such ominous effect.

Student residences are situated in the side wings of the building. There is no difference between the Russian and the Yugoslav students, except that instead of delivering milk, Russian students work as stokers and night-watchmen. Some say the number of abortion cases among girl students is very high. You see many Negro and Asian faces. Relations with the Negroes have been very tense, especially since their demonstrations in Red Square last winter. "They sent us only bourgeois students," complained my official guide, Oleg Merkurov, a nice Siberian.

In spite of constant threats that they will be sent to "work colonies" for a year or two, the students are not afraid to discuss everything openly. They unhesitatingly criticize all the shortcomings of their country. True, one still encounters a certain amount of mutual suspicion. Thus, a student with whom I became very friendly warned me that another student in our group was a *stukach,* a stoolpigeon. A few days later, the alleged stoolpigeon told me the same thing about my friend. But the students are all great optimists and they all feel that life is better and freer every day. I was surprised that nobody paid any attention to the groups standing on stairways and loudly singing prison and concentration camp songs.

Through foreign students—about a thousand of them—the MGU receives the Western press and Western books and records, ending the severe isolation that existed before. Jazz of all kinds is extremely popular. Since records are very expensive, tapes are constantly being made. This in spite of a semi-official campaign against jazz (twist records are confiscated from Soviet citizens at the border). Not so long ago, however, the radio program *Yunost (Youth)* was founded and jazz is often heard on its broadcasts. As is true everywhere, the students favor the avant-garde in all fields.

I have met young and unknown poets who are admirers of the Symbolist poet Andrei Bely (who has still not been republished) and worshipers of Malevich's abstractions. I have talked to students intimately familiar with Kafka, and I have even met admirers of Nabokov's *Lolita.* There was only one kind I did not meet among the MGU students: I did not meet a single admirer of dogmatic Socialist Realism.

THE LITERARY SITUATION

The basic characteristic of the Soviet literary mood in the summer of 1964 was the expectation of a final liberation of literature and arts from all possible restrictions of dogmatic Marxism.[2] One felt this not only in the pages of magazines and newspapers, but in contacts with eminent Soviet writers and editors as well. "A new 1956 is coming," a well-known Soviet writer told me.

A new novel by Vladimir Dudintsev was expected. A new edition of collected works of Pasternak was in preparation—but without his *Dr. Zhivago*. Kafka's *The Trial* was being prepared for print. Soviet critics write more often now, and quite positively, about Kafka's works. The magazine *Voprosy Literatury* [*Questions of Literature*] (No. 5, 1964) contained an interesting, voluminous and serious study by D. Zatonsky, "Kafka without Retouching." Zatonsky had already written an article on Kafka in the magazine *Inostrannaya Literatura* [*Foreign Literature*] (No. 2, 1959), "The Death and Birth of Franz Kafka." With the publication of *Metamorphosis* and other Kafka novels in *Inostrannaya Literatura* (No. 1, 1964), and the Ukrainian translation of *The Trial*, he has been able to offer a much broader and more scholarly

[2] Since the summer of 1964, of course, there has occurred not "a final liberation of literature" but the toppling of Khrushchev with an essential, though less histrionic, continuation of his hostile, Philistine attitude toward writers.

treatment of the great writer, and can be followed by Soviet readers.

Zatonsky's "Kafka without Retouching" starts by ridiculing and rejecting the "Zhdanovian" attitude toward Kafka: "The Albanian weekly *Drita* has expressed disapproval because at one of our scholarly conferences in Moscow one of the participants 'dared' analyze the works of decadent writers, especially Kafka. Such hardened sectarianism can provoke only an ironical smile on the lips of any right-thinking man. If literature is to be understood, if literature is to be created, it is essential to explain its history in all its aspects—the near and the distant, the healthy and the unhealthy. Kafka hated that cruel dehumanized world in which he lived, he hated it deeply and with passion. He described the unrelieved horror of human existence in the 'penal colony' of bourgeois civilization; he has suffered for man and felt responsible for him. One cannot but feel sympathy with his search and his grief."

Zatonsky surveys the critical works on Kafka with which he is well acquainted, citing in the bibliography some 26 studies, from Max Brod to Günter Anders and Robbe-Grillet; he continues by analyzing one by one all of Kafka's works. But the study brings no new discoveries, and it concludes in a very acceptable manner: "The Kafka tradition lies outside the mainstream of the artistic development of the epoch. Strange is the sad destiny of Kafka, stranger than his creative work itself—this testimonial against the contemporary bourgeois world, against contemporary bourgeois culture. In its own way, Kafka's destiny represents both a lesson and a warning." Thus Zatonsky obediently repeats the untenable thesis that Kafka was connected with capitalistic society, while the truth is exactly the contrary: Kafka was a horrified prophet of the totalitarian, bureaucratized society. I still think, nevertheless, that the appearance of this voluminous work represents an important step toward breaking up the existing "ideological frontiers."

Many of the writers and critics with whom I spoke, especially those of the younger generation and the graduate students at the MGU, are literally crazy about Kafka. In Yugoslavia, Kafka has never inspired such enthusiasm. It would seem, therefore, that the appearance of a great number of Russian "Kafkaites" may be expected very soon.

Many other classics of Western literature are also being translated. In 1963, a collection of Rimbaud's poems was published. Hemingway's *For Whom the Bell Tolls* is in preparation. Surprisingly, the most popular and respected writer among the general public is Somerset Maugham. Thomas Mann—the only modern "great" whose works have almost all been translated into Russian (except for *Joseph and His Brothers*)—has not provoked much interest.

Unfortunately, there is no talk about the possibility of translating T. S. Eliot, Joyce, D. H. Lawrence, Henry James, Proust, Virginia Woolf, Malaparte, Beckett, Ionesco, Camus, Hesse and other great artists of our time. And the situation is the same in the field of philosophy and social science, where one does not hear such names as Georg Lukacs, Freud, Lucien Goldmann, Ernst Bloch, Erich Fromm, not to mention Karl Jaspers, Martin Heidegger or Emmanuel Mounier. Happily, though, I found that many young Soviet scientists and several outstanding students were reading these authors in their original language. But it is extremely difficult to obtain their books, and when available they are sold at high prices. (I saw an edition of Joyce's *Ulysses* that was purchased for 10 rubles [about $11].)

The most popular Russian writer these days is Aleksandr Solzhenitsyn. I was told that in the last year alone there were four graduate theses about Solzhenitsyn in the MGU Philosophy Department.

This year's Lenin prize, however, was given to the Ukrainian writer Oles Gonchar for his "novel in novelettes," *Tronka*. Gonchar is the typical *"lakirovshchik"* ["lacquering man"].[3] He is a neo-Socialist Realist, who depicts a rosy life in a *kolkhoz* where all the conflicts are on the level of a children's quarrel and always end in reconciliation. We see that even a former inspector in one of Stalin's concentration camps, retired now with a big pension which enables him to buy a car, realizes his "mistake" from the time of the "cult":

" 'It happens that I cannot sleep at night, thinking: What kind of magic was that? What was that bloody eclipse obsessing all of us? How could we pray only to him, to this idol of ours, how could we trust him?'

[3] This term neatly combines the concepts of forced optimism and crude workmanship.

" 'Yes, that's how it was,' agreed Dorsokhenko. 'A shame! A shame before the whole world.

" 'They, the young ones, they think that all this is so simple: The fathers are bad, the fathers are the "cult people," while we are clean, we are angels. We shall see what will become of these angels. To dance to the music is one thing, but to live . . .' "

The whole book is godawfully wretched. There is no evidence of any talent in *Tronka*.

On the other hand, one notes many rehabilitations of the once-suppressed and excommunicated modernists and émigrés. If this trend continues, and all signs suggest it will, the day is not far off when the Association of Soviet Writers and the Association of Russian Writers in Paris, once presided over by the famous novelist Boris Zaitsev, will merge. In the magazine *Moskva* (No. 1, 1964), Pilnyak was rehabilitated and one of his hitherto unknown short stories was published. *Moskva* has also published reminiscences of Nikolai Chukovsky on Osip Mandelstam, along with some of Mandelstam's poems.[4] The magazine *Znamya* (No. 8, 1964) has brought to light some unpublished stories by Isaac Babel.

The rise in popularity of Nikolai Gumilyov (1886–

[4] A translation of this fragment of Nikolai Chukovsky's memoirs—he is the son of the famed elderly writer Kornei Chukovsky—appeared in the same issue of the Yugoslav *Delo* as Mihajlov's article. Although to date only a few such excerpts from the memoirs have appeared in various Soviet journals, those who have attended private readings from the book by Chukovsky declare that these reminiscences far surpass those of Paustovsky and Ehrenburg in terms both of intrinsic literary merit and of their importance as a chronicle of 20th century Russian culture.

1921), the great Russian poet, is considerable. His poetry is now in print and I have heard enthusiastic eulogies of Gumilyov by young student poets. In our country this poet is almost unknown, although together with Mayakovsky, Tsvetaeva and Esenin, he was one of the most significant Russian poets of the '20s. Gumilyov, a leader of the Acmeist movement, was the husband of Anna Akhmatova. He was shot in 1921 for participating in a counterrevolutionary conspiracy, and was therefore ignored in his own country until recently. In the 1952 edition of the Great Soviet Encyclopedia Gumilyov's name was not mentioned. Yet Gumilyov was a vital, masculine personality. He graduated from the Sorbonne, headed two expeditions in Africa, founded the "Russian Society for Lion Hunting," volunteered in World War I, and fought actively against Soviet authority. Gumilyov's poetry has strength and vital energy; it glorifies courageous conquistadors, invaders, sailors, all who every day fearlessly face death. His present popularity among the Soviet youth is revealing. It was Gumilyov's own fearless and brazen attitude while being interrogated by the Leningrad *Cheka* that provoked his inquisitors to fury and moved them to liquidate him posthaste when they heard that Gorky had met with Lenin and received assurances that Gumilyov would not be shot. Here is how Evgeny Zamyatin tells the story:

"It happened that on my way back from Moscow to Petersburg I was traveling in the same car with Gorky, not long before his departure [from Russia—M.M.]. It was night, and all the passengers were sleeping. For quite a while we were standing in the corridor, watching the sparks through the window, and talking. We talked of the great Russian poet Gumilyov, who was shot a few months before. . . . He was a man alien to Gorky both in politics and literature, yet in spite of this Gorky did all he could in trying to save him. According to Gorky, he had been promised in Moscow that Gumilyov's life would be spared, but the Petersburg authorities somehow heard of this and hastened to execute his sentence. I never saw Gorky so excited."

Evgeny Zamyatin and Remizov are still on the blacklist, but I was surprised by the fact that many people were familiar with them nonetheless.

A recent flood of books about Dostoevsky is also revealing. More and more new and interesting critics are appearing, such as Chirkov and Tsudnelovich. A new edition of the complete works of Dostoevsky is in preparation. One critical volume that stirred up a controversy was M. M. Bakhtin's *The Problems of Dostoevsky's Poetics* (Moscow, 1963), which actually is a revised and enlarged edition of his *The Problems of Dostoevsky's Art* (published in 1922). Bakhtin is a follower of the so-called "formalistic school" in science and literature, and his book is of particular value in the field of the theory of the novel. But since the formalists were suppressed for decades, this eminent scholar was forced to go into a sort of exile at the University of Sarinsk, capital city of the Moldavian autonomous republic, where he still lives.

Bakhtin's rehabilitation followed his recent publication in Italy. Since every rehabilitation provokes a contrary reaction, his book was soon attacked by the veteran "official arbiter" Dymshits in *Literaturnaya Gazeta* [*Literary Newspaper*]. Significantly, this time Dymshits was countered by almost all of the most eminent Soviet critics: Asmus, Pertsov, Shklovsky, Krapchenko, Vasylevskaya and Myasnikov (also in *Literaturnaya Gazeta*). Even V. Ermilov, the ill-reputed theoretician of strict Socialist Realism, defended Bakhtin. This shows that the strength of the Russian Renaissance has grown to such an extent that even the most stubborn Socialist Realists have started to go over to the opposite camp.

During my stay in Moscow there appeared still another heavy volume on Dostoevsky by G. M. Friedlander. Interestingly, too, even Svetlana Sarukhanova, Komsomol Secretary of the Leningrad University, spoke with enthusiasm about the great author and took me to the Dostoevsky room in the Writers' Museum. This rise in Dostoevsky's popularity is quite understandable. The 20th Party Congress destroyed a long-standing myth; it also confused many people in the process, robbed them of their psychic support and created a number of lost beings who are not unlike Dostoevsky's "heroes."

In contrast, I was surprised by the attitude toward Sholokhov and Leonov held by most of the young people I met. They do not count them among the living writers. "These men are only monuments," I was told by one student, who added: "In the past, before the War, Sholokhov was an artist . . ."

On the other hand, the modern Soviet mystic, Aleksandr

Grin, is very popular among the youth. Recently I read in the *Literaturnaya Gazeta* that Grin was published in millions of copies, far more than the total for any other Russian writers of either the 19th or 20th centuries. Born in a remote Russian province, Grin (1880–1932) had a difficult life as worker, tramp, professional revolutionary, soldier of the civil war, etc. In his novels and stories he created a strange world of fantasy, a world in which justice and beauty triumph, in which the sun is always shining and good people are rewarded by happiness. His novels and stories are distinguished by adventurous plots enacted in mythical places such as "Gel-Gyul," "Zurbagan," and "Liss." Everything is invented and unreal, except the very palpable reality of human imagination.

"Man has a right not to see that which objectively exists, but that which he wishes to see." These words, uttered by a heroine in the most significant Grin novel, *She Who Runs on Waves*, might serve as the theme of all his works. Grin's world is strange because everything ends happily and the sun is always shining, but also because the basic motivations of his characters are determined by intuition, telepathy, clairvoyance and other parapsychological phenomena. The recent founding of the Research Institute for Parapsychological Phenomena of the Academy of Medical Science of the USSR suggests, though, that Grin's work may be closer to reality (or to surreality) than was thought.

For many years Grin was on the blacklist. Little of his work was published, and if his name was mentioned, it was only for the purpose of attacking him, as in articles like V. Vazhdaev's "Preacher of Cosmopolitanism" in *Novy Mir* (No. 1, 1950), or Tarasenkov's "On National Traditions and Bourgeois Cosmopolitanism" in *Znamya* (No. 1, 1950). The following appeared in the 1952 Great Soviet Encyclopedia:

"In his works after the October period Grin puts forth against the Soviet reality a certain imaginary land with the nonexistent exotic cities of Zurbagan and Gel-Gyul, an unnational, cosmopolitan paradise of sorts. By glorifying the Nietzschean type of 'Superman,' Grin tendentiously portrays his heroes as 'aristocrats of spirit,' men without a fatherland—as opposed to the people, depicted in his works as sinister, stupid and crude, incapable of creative activity. Reactionary-mystic ideas of Grin's are mostly constructed in adventurous detective plots."

But times are changing. Only five years later, in the 1957 edition of *Collected Works of A. Grin*, Konstantin Paustovsky writes: "The world in which Grin's heroes live may seem unreal only to a man of poor spirit . . . Grin has populated his books with a tribe of daring, proud, self-sacrificing and good people. Only a blind man will fail to see a love of mankind in Grin's books. He wrote of our ignorance of nature, of its power. . . ."[5]

Along with the imaginary world of Grin, any kind of science-fiction is extremely popular. But it is difficult to buy a science-fiction novel anywhere; enormous editions

[5] Since Mihajlov wrote this article Grin's short story, "The Rat-Catcher," has been republished for the first time in the Soviet Union. This brilliant work about a man trapped in a maze-like building, a work which predates Kafka, is classic "Kafkaesque" fiction.

are sold out within hours after publication. The most widely read writer in this field currently is Isaac Asimov, an American whom the Russians have recently started to publish.

It is often hard, in fact, to obtain any good book. The most interesting works, owing to ideological controls still effective, are published in extremely small editions, except for science-fiction. Thus, the famous Dudintsev novel *Not By Bread Alone* was published in 30,000 copies; Bakhtin's book on Dostoevsky, 9,500; the book of the modern art theoretician Turbin, which caused so much debate, 22,000; and a book of collected works of Bertolt Brecht in only 5,000 copies. But the growing younger generation of scholars will undoubtedly change this situation. I asked a certain MGU student specializing in contemporary Western European literature when Joyce and Proust will be published in the Soviet Union. He answered: "If it were up to me, they would be published tomorrow." And this is the view held everywhere among the younger generation. When you talk to a professor, you are dealing with one world; when you talk with an assistant to the same professor, you are dealing with quite another. The only question concerning complete liberalization seems to be how long it will take.

The essence of Zhdanovism lies not in the demand that art be realistic rather than modernistic, but in the insistence that art be uniform. I believe that the dogmatists would rather accept a uniform modernism than allow even a small number of artists to separate themselves from the rigid Socialist Realist line.

The famous critic from the first decade after October, Aleksandr Voronsky, spoke about precisely this problem in January 1925, at the First All-Union Writers' Conference: "They wish to stand with a stick in their hands waving it over your heads. Those who stand slightly taller than the rest would have their heads knocked off. With this same stick they will dictate your theme, idea, style. I fear that in a few years' time literature will become as heartless as an account book. Novels and poems will be produced according to prescribed measures. Idylls and odes will be written on strict orders, regardless of reality, regardless of artistic truth."

The fact that Voronsky's fears were justified was confirmed by Mikhail Sholokhov, who said in February 1956: "And thus it all started. Fadeev showed himself as a rather power-thirsty Secretary General . . . to work with him was impossible. This state of affairs lasted for fifteen years . . . And don't you think that Fadeev could have been told in time: 'The thirst for power is an unnecessary thing in the literary profession. The Writers' Union is not a military detachment, and in any case it is not a penitential detachment, so not a single writer will stand at "attention" in front of you, Comrade Fadeev.'" Unfortunately, this same Sholokhov today willingly allows the founding of an Institute for Studies of the Life and Work of Mikhail Sholokhov in Rostov-on-the-Don, and permits his name to be exploited in every possible way in the Soviet press.

Although the current situation cannot even be compared to that of ten years ago, there still are official standards of Socialist Realism obligatory for all members of the Writers' Union. (True, these standards are now much more elastic than before.) An article by V. Chalmaev in the magazine *Kommunist* (No. 8, 1964), "The Hero and the Heroic in Soviet Literature," showed that the strength of militant dogmatism is still very great. In Moscow, several older professors at the MGU enthusiastically urged me to read Chalmaev's article. In spite of this, the followers of Socialist Realism are in an unenviable position nowadays, for the very term "Socialist Realism" is associated with Stalin. In 1958, the Soviet writer Valery Ozerov[6] gave the following description of the birth of Socialist Realism: "There were frequent discussions at this time [early thirties—M.M.] about the characteristics of Soviet literature. The many-sided exchange of views was concluded in Gorky's apartment on October 26, 1932, when the words 'Socialist Realism,' which were to be generally accepted later on, were heard for the first time. They were uttered that evening by Stalin, and they have crowned and concluded the collective thinking and searching of the artists."

A special, extremely important factor in the present state of literary affairs is the conflict with China. In August, the Chinese press attacked several young poets—Voznesensky, Evtushenko, Akhmadulina—in the same words with which they were condemned at the "historic"

[6] Ozerov is the Editor of the journal *Questions of Literature*. Ozerov is mentioned several times in Mihajlov's essay, never favorably. It subsequently developed that Ozerov had visited Yugoslavia and, upon his return to Moscow, had printed a harsh and very reactionary attack upon the journal *Delo* in which Mihajlov's essay appeared.

meeting of the Party with the writers in the spring of 1963. But after the Chinese attack, *Izvestia* started defending the poets in the very words the poets themselves had used to rebut the attacks of party ideologist Leonid Ilichyov in 1963. And generally speaking, the Soviet-Chinese polemic serves nowadays as the best weapon in the struggle against orthodox domestic Zhdanovism.

The climate is thus favorable for freeing artistic forces, and all the young people are optimistic regarding the future. The most vivid contemporary Russian literature is represented by the young poets—Andrei Voznesensky, Evgeny Evtushenko, Bella Akhmadulina, Rimma Kazakova, Novella Matveeva, Yuna Morits, Robert Rozhdestvensky, Tamara Zhirmunskaya, Viktor Sosnora—and by such older poets as Evgeny Vinokurov and Bulat Okudzhava. Leonid Martynov is the group's recognized chorus leader, but he is already fifty years old. In prose works, in addition to the older writers—Solzhenitsyn, Dudintsev and the aged Paustovsky—the group of young writers of the sixties includes Vladimir Tendryakov, Yury Kazakov, Sergei Nikitin, Natalya Tarasenkova, Iosif Dik, Pavel Nilin and Vil Lipatov. Every day new talents appear, exciting for the courage with which they handle "painful" themes of Soviet society.

There has been a gradual disappearance of incidents such as the ban and withdrawal of *Pages from Tarusa,* a collection of pieces that included contributions from Paustovsky, Okudzhava, Zabolotsky, Tsvetaeva and many other prominent authors. Publication of the book, which appeared in 1961 in an edition of 75,000, had been greeted by the public as a major event in Soviet literature.[7]

In 1921 Evgeny Zamyatin wrote:

"In essence, real literature can exist only where it is created not by careful and loyal functionaries, but by maniacs, hermits, day-dreamers, rebels, skeptics. And if the writer has to be loyal, if he must be orthodox like a Catholic, if he may not lash out at everyone like Swift, and if he may not laugh at everything like Anatole France, then there will be no literature engraved on bronze tablets but only paper—newspapers which we read today, and wrap soap in tomorrow. . . . I am afraid that there will be no real literature in our country as long as they do not stop looking at the Russian *demos* as at a child whose virginity one has to defend. I am afraid there will be no real literature in our country as long as we are not cured of the new Catholicism which, no less than the old one, fears every heretical word. And if this illness is incurable, I am afraid that Russian literature has only one future: its past."[8]

---

[7] Before the book's withdrawal an estimated 8,000 to 10,000 copies had been sold. Contrary to some reports published in the West, the withdrawal order on *Pages from Tarusa* was not rescinded—copies were made available to writers in the special bookstores reserved for members of the Writers' Union, but not to the "general reading public."

[8] This citation is from Zamyatin's article entitled "I Am Afraid," which was published in Russia in 1920. Like the previous Zamyatin passage it was taken from a Russian-language edition of Zamyatin's critical articles published in New York in 1955. Zamyatin, after a campaign of vilification against him, unexpectedly received permission to leave the Soviet Union in 1931, after addressing a bold request to Stalin himself. His anti-utopian novel *We* was branded a "libel on the socialist future." Zamyatin died in France in 1937.

The young Soviet generation, with its uncompromising "hereticism," gives us hope that the future of Russian literature will not be in its past.

ACADEMICIAN NIKOLAI GUDZY

Near Red Square and the Philosophic Faculty, right in the center of Moscow, at 10 Granovsky Street, lives the Academician Nikolai K. Gudzy, the most famous and most important scholar of Russian literature. His voluminous *History of Russian Literature* has had six editions in the Soviet Union and has been translated into several foreign languages. My meeting with Gudzy was arranged by the International Department of the MGU—the first in a series of visits with prominent Russian literati.

Gudzy's apartment was filled to the ceiling with books, so that you could not see a patch of wall in any of his rooms (he claims to have more than 10,000). The amiable old man, a long-time professor at Moscow University, proudly showed me some rare and valuable editions of Aleksei Remizov, Evgeny Zamyatin, and Andrei Bely. It was with special pride that he showed me a letter from the "Russian Kafka," Remizov, sent to him from Paris a few days before Remizov's death. Shortly before his death

Remizov became completely blind; the letter had been written by his wife and signed by Remizov.

At Gudzy's place I also saw for the first time the well-known monograph on Remizov by Natalya Kodryanskaya, published in Paris in 1959. All this only confirmed my belief that contemporary Russian historians and critics are reading émigré literature, and that some day they will write about it.

Gudzy kindly offered to give me the telephone numbers of some of the Moscow writers, giving me the idea of contacting some of them personally. Later I learned from Professor Balakin, a lecturer in Yugoslav literature at the MGU, that he once was asked by Gudzy to translate one of my essays on *Anna Karenina* in which I had attacked him: The worthy historian Gudzy seemed to take offense and decided to write a sharp reply, which was published in the magazine *Russkaya Literatura*. My host did not mention this to me.

MIKHAILOVSKY IN UZKOE

A few miles from the last station of the *Novye Cheryo-myshki* subway line, running east from the center of Moscow, lies the sanatorium of the Academy of Science of the USSR—"Uzkoe." It is situated in a classical Russian setting of cheerless birch forests and small artificial lakes. The vast 18th-century building, in the style of Turgenev's "nobleman's nest" with Doric columns at the main entrance, is used by the Soviet academicians for rest and vacations and as a place to work. There I visited Boris Mikhailovsky, the famed literary historian and critic who was recuperating from two heart attacks.

Like all other scholars with whom I have talked, Milkhailovsky is a great optimist regarding the rehabilitation of the Russian modernists. He told me the Academy of Science was preparing the third tome of the *History of Russian Literature from 1890 to 1917*, in which Bely, Leonid Andreev and Remizov will be treated in detail.[9] In 1939, Mikhailovsky wrote a book entitled *Russian Literature of the Twentieth Century* which, in spite of numerous omissions and shortcomings, played a helpful role at a time when a mention of the Symbolists was inadmissible.

Academician Mikhailovsky, a courteous elderly gentleman with a Chekhovian beard, told me that since childhood he had dreamed of visiting Yugoslavia. "If I were asked what foreign country I would like to visit, I would say Yugoslavia," he told me while we were making a tour of the sanatorium and inspecting originals by Repin and other Russian artists whose pictures fill the walls. The

[9] The *History of Russian Literature from 1890 to 1917* has since appeared, and we must assume that the volume fell victim to the censor's pencil, for it is, in fact, most disappointing—none of the three writers mentioned by Mikhailovsky [is] treated in detail, and Remizov is not discussed at all.

term "sanatorium" does not seem to fit the place, since nothing there is reminiscent of a hospital. It looks much more like a hotel or a luxurious private club. In this house, Mikhailovsky told me, the great Russian philosopher Vladimir Solovyov once lived.

THE SEARCH FOR GOLOSOVKER

Even before I started for Moscow I had decided to find Yakov Emanuilovich Golosovker. In 1963, the Academy of Science of the USSR published a booklet entitled *Dostoevsky and Kant* which stood out among the numerous recent Soviet works on Dostoevsky. The author was new to me, and the book was extraordinary.

The first man whom I asked about Golosovker was the dean of the Faculty of Philosophy, Dr. Solovyov. He had never heard of Golosovker. Academician Mikhailovsky had heard of him, but he had a curious smile on his face when he spoke of him; he told me that Golosovker was a very strange man and that he was a philosopher, not a man of letters. He did not know his address. Academician Gudzy knew the address. He warned me that Golosovker was an incommunicative and queer person who had spent a long time in a concentration camp, an impossible man who never accepts any compromise and has strange ideas.

Since I already knew and agreed with Golosovker's ideas, I was all the more eager to see him after what I was told by the distinguished academicians.

For several days I tried to call Golosovker by phone. There was no answer. I then went to his apartment (luckily, not far away from my hotel at Lenin's Hills). Nobody opened the door. I returned the next day, again in vain. I knocked at the door of his neighbors and learned that the tenant one floor above might have the address of Golosovker's nephew, who would certainly know the whereabouts of his uncle. From the woman who told me this I also discovered that Golosovker was an old man with a long white beard. While reading his book, I had thought the writer a young man, so bold and challenging were his ideas. The upstairs tenant was not at home, and was out again the next day. The third time I succeeded, and got the telephone number of Golosovker's nephew.

Then I started all over again with the telephone. Nobody answered at first. After several tries at various times, a feminine voice answered (I found out later that she was the maid) and told me that the nephew, Sigurt Otovich Shmidt, had gone to his *dacha,* where there was no telephone; that she did not know when he would be back; that Golosovker was in the hospital and she had no right to tell me the name of the hospital, even if I were from the moon and not merely from Yugoslavia. All my persuasion was in vain. I could not get the name of the hospital. And there are many hospitals in Moscow.

That was the end; I could try nothing else. I called both numbers from time to time, in vain. There was no answer at Golosovker's apartment, and his nephew was still at his *dacha*. Yet my desire to see the strange philosopher now was growing precisely because his whereabouts were being hidden from me.

On the last day of my stay in Moscow I unexpectedly reached Comrade Shmidt, the nephew, as I made my final routine call to his apartment. He was extremely polite but said Yakov Emanuilovich was seriously ill and visits were prohibited. I still do not understand why he did not want to give me the name of the hospital, since I would not have been admitted there if visitors were prohibited.

Golosovker, Sigurt Otovich told me, was 74 years old and had led a lonely existence all his life. He graduated from the University of Kiev, was a classicist by education, and between the two wars had published many translations of ancient lyrics, a complete Pindar as well as Hölderlin. Anatoly Lunacharsky wrote with much praise about him. He was imprisoned in a camp for a short while, Comrade Shmidt told me: only five years!

The booklet *Dostoevsky and Kant* is only a small part of his work on Dostoevsky. Let us hope that the rest of it will be published some day, even if the author is "a queer man who never accepts any compromise."[10] Of all the plans and all the hopes I failed to realize in Russia, the

[10] One of the most striking things about Golosovker's book is its complete absence of any ceremonial bows to Marx and Lenin.

one I am saddest about is not meeting with Golosovker. By all signs he appears to be an unusual man and an important philosopher.

VLADIMIR DUDINTSEV

Vladimir Dudintsev! In Soviet literature this name is a symbol of 1956. I remember with what impatience and expectation I read his novel, *Not By Bread Alone,* since this was the first Russian book translated in Yugoslavia after 1948. And I still remember my original disappointment. The book was nothing special; an ordinary realistic novel about an engineer fighting for the acceptance of his invention. I couldn't understand why such a big fuss had been made about it in the Soviet Union. What was most surprising, though, was that the Americans had made two pictures based on this novel, and that it was translated into eighteen languages in record time.

Much, much later, while reading the novel a second time, I realized that beneath the unspectacular fable form of this "production novel"[11] there was hidden an authentic, contemporary tragedy of Soviet society. That is, the tragedy of a talented individual who has to stake his

[11] Mihajlov alludes here to the distressing phenomenon in which the puerile form of the "triumphant-labor-for-the-Party" novel intrudes itself upon much "liberal" Soviet writing.

life to realize his original idea—a mere technical idea, which makes the tragedy all the greater. One is forced to ask: What would have happened to a man trying to give the world a new idea of another kind—philosophical, political, social?

Eventually people wrote much less about Dudintsev. In 1960 his short story, "New Year's Tale," was published and translated into six languages, but his name was not mentioned again in the Soviet press. Only in June 1964, amid the arguments over a short story by the young Siberian writer Vil Lipatov, did Dudintsev's name appear beneath an article in *Literaturnaya Gazeta*. So he exists, I thought, and decided to visit him.

One day about 9 P.M. (in Moscow, in June, the day lasts almost until midnight), I entered the huge building at 19 Lomonosov Prospect, not far from the MGU. (Only writers live in the whole enormous building, I learned later; in Number 14, a still bigger building on the same street, the tenants are all university professors.) Somehow, that same day, I had stayed on at a lunch party at number 14 which lasted until 9 P.M., and had, alas, drunk more vodka than I could take, not being accustomed to the mammoth dimensions of the glasses. And so it happened that I came to see Dudintsev slightly warmed by "*Stolichnaya*" (Capital City) Vodka (luckily, Number 19 was not far away from Number 14) and spent the whole evening talking passionately about everything, but mostly about Yugoslavia. I did not give my host a chance to say more than a dozen or so words. I told him about the Adriatic Sea, and about the Workers' Councils, about Yugoslavia's rotation of office holders, and much more, including the fact that in Yugoslavia we may read both the Western and the Eastern press.

Dudintsev only asked questions and repeated several times: "Yes, yes, of course, you are in the avant-garde!" I left him around midnight extremely satisfied, and it was not until the next morning that I fell into a deep depression when I realized that I had wanted to see him in order to ask him questions, but had instead not even given him a chance to say a few words. I called him up again, excused myself for my verbosity the night before and expressed my deep regret at missing my chance to learn something from him about his plans and work. Dudintsev was very nice, and invited me to visit him again whenever I felt like it. And so I did.

Dudintsev is a short man with a big oval head and clever, lively eyes behind thick glasses. He is as gay and direct as a child, and does not resemble the portrait in the Serbo-Croatian edition of his novel. Every now and then he would get up from his chair, go to his desk and scribble something. Without hesitation I would say that he is one of the most honest people I met in Moscow.

He lives with his wife and three daughters, who are in high school, and leads a very modest life. In order to survive he has to translate from Ukrainian much of the time, together with his wife. Authors' fees in the USSR are relatively high, enabling a number of poets to live off the publication of one small collection of poems per year (as, for instance, is the case with Evgeny Vinokurov). But Dudintsev, like so many other "disobedient" writers, hardly manages to make both ends meet—disobedient writers' works are published in the smallest possible editions. Dudintsev showed me a typewritten copy of his novel that somebody had sent him from the provinces; this is probably the only 20th century novel which is being distributed in typewritten form.

"I need only four and a half months of free time to finish my new novel," complained the author. Its title is *The Unknown Soldier* and it deals with the conflict of the biologists—the followers of Lysenko and the so-called Morganists—when the latter were being sent to concentration camps for "biological deviations" in 1948. Since Dudintsev is obliged to translate to earn a living, he has to keep postponing the completion of his novel.

Not long ago Dudintsev's German publisher visited him in Moscow and was astonished by the poverty evidenced by the author's apartment. "I thought you were the richest man in Russia," the publisher told him. For in spite of the fact that Soviet Russia has not signed the International Copyright Convention, many Western publishers were paying huge royalties for publishing Dudintsev's novel to *Mezhdunarodnaya Kniga* [Soviet International Book Organization] with whom Dudintsev had an agreement—70 per cent of the royalties to him, and 30 per cent to *Mezhdunarodnaya Kniga*. *Mezhdunarodnaya Kniga* was not sticking to the contract, however, and Dudintsev had not received a cent from them. "Now that's what I call capitalistic exploitation!" the author's German publisher told him.

Still, like all other Russian writers, Dudintsev was optimistic, believing that a new liberalization wave was imminent, "a new 1956," and he cited certain symptoms which he had noted lately. Thus, Vsevolod Kochetov, editor of the ultra-conservative magazine *October* and a writer who had attacked Dudintsev fervently before, now publicly offered to publish his new novel *The Unknown Soldier* in *October*. Kochetov's gesture is significant, for he is known as a stubbornly orthodox Socialist Realist and was recently praised by Chinese literary critics, who called him almost the only revolutionary writer today. Kochetov felt the need to back away from the Chinese praise. He stated that he was following the general line of Soviet writers and that he was sticking with the others, so he offered a hand of reconciliation to Dudintsev.

"The dogmatists are not the worst ones," Dudintsev told me. "They are at least honest in their own way. The worst are those who have no ideas of their own and who stay with the old boat until the last moment, leaving it only when the new boat is near enough. They hate to swim and they fight to evade this. You see, it is not clear to them why the weeds are growing again when it seemed that *October* had ploughed the earth so deeply that the land became sterile."

Remembering all the noise from 1956, the writer told me that his most important, his greatest experience was when people unknown to him, in a bus or in the subway, without looking him in the eyes, secretly squeezed his hand. "For this it's worthwhile to endure anything," he told me.

Unlike Ilya Ehrenburg and Leonid Leonov, Dudintsev has a positive opinion of the new generation in Soviet literature. Like many others he considers Novella Matveeva, a young woman in poor health who lives virtually for and from poetry, as the most significant phenomenon in poetry. He read me Matveeva's poem "The Lighthouse," full of deep symbolism and written in a juicy and original Russian idiom, a quality seldom found nowadays in the poetry of the young, especially in the case of Evtushenko. Dudintsev read with inspiration, and one could feel that he associated the last verses with his own destiny:

Somebody with a thought of a thief
vainly skulks
along the shore at night;
he wants your fire,
as if with his hand
to close your mouth
and shout
"Enough! Shut up!"
But you speak with fire.
So clearly,
that in the moist darkness,
in misty distance,
you will be seen
and heard
and the ships
will not mistake you.

Dudintsev did not have the opportunity to read Pasternak's *Dr. Zhivago*. Before I left, he told me: "I would like to visit Yugoslavia." The way things are developing in the Soviet Union today his novel *Not By Bread Alone* will undoubtedly be noisily rehabilitated soon, and will be reprinted in quantity. The words of the critic Valery Ozerov, written in 1958, already sound very comical: "Yes, in our country some works emerged which were quite deservedly condemned by Soviet public opinion. Following 'critical dramas,' which presented the leading cadres of the Soviet state as stubborn bureaucrats, the novel of V. Dudintsev, *Not By Bread Alone*, has come into the light of day. In this book, no place could be found for depicting the creative activity of the Party, while instead, the all-powerful functionaries were very much present. . . . Naturally, such works will be completely forgotten very soon, but one must bear in mind how dangerous even the smallest underestimation of the theme of the Party is under present conditions."

TAMARA ZHIRMUNSKAYA

Of the young poets, Evtushenko and Rozhdestvensky were off at the North Sea, Rimma Kazakova somewhere in the South, Yuna Morits and Novella Matveeva "in *dacha*"—leaving only Voznesensky and Zhirmunskaya in

Moscow. I telephoned Zhirmunskaya. She told me to come over whenever it was convenient for me since she was home all the time. She was expecting a baby.

Tamara Zhirmunskaya was born in 1936. Like most of the younger poets and writers, she is a graduate of the Maxim Gorky Institute for Literature in Moscow— headed by one of the greatest masters of Russian prose of our time, Konstantin Paustovsky. After completing her studies, she traveled extensively through the country as a newspaper reporter and made frequent appearances at poetry discussions and readings. Though not as talented as Akhmadulina and Matveeva, her poems appeal to the widest readership because of their simplicity and lyricism. Her basic theme is the expectation of happiness, and characteristically, the title of one of her collections is *The District of My Love.*

In an old house "from Tsarist times" on Gorky Street, in an apartment crowded with antique furniture (the dwellings of Chekhov's intelligentsia must have looked just like this), a massive blonde woman whom you would never have taken for a poet showed me photographs of many gatherings of young people, Evtushenko, Rozhdestvensky, Voznesensky, herself . . . and crowds of people. She told me the public was so eager for something new, that if 10 complete unknowns put up a poster announcing an evening of poetry, that would suffice to fill up the theater. Naturally, such a potential reception "acts as an inspiration," she said, and that is the real "social task"—a very precise and useful term, unfortunately compromised and in ill repute because it was always identified with a task assigned by the Ideological Committee of the Central Committee of the Communist Party of the Soviet Union.

Soon Zhirmunskaya's husband arrived, an editor of a film magazine. This enabled me to learn many interesting things about the situation in the Soviet cinema.

FILMS

Zhirmunskaya's husband told me the whole story of the film *The Gate of Ilich* (the name of one of Moscow's districts). Three years ago, director Marlen Khutsev made a picture based on a screenplay by Genady Shtolikov which centered around the conflict of the younger Soviet generation with its fathers. Everyone invited to special screenings said it was a masterpiece. The Party Commission, however, refused to allow its release because "there is no conflict between fathers and their children in our country." Khrushchev was revolted by the film, particularly by the final scene, which contained the essence of the work. In that scene, the hero, a contemporary Soviet youth, has got himself into a difficult situation, and at night dreams that he is in a bunker during the War, talking to his father on the very evening before the assault in which his father lost his life. The youth asks his father: "Father, what should I do?"

The father replies: "My son, how old are you?"

"Twenty-three, father."

"Then why are you asking me, since I am only 21?" replies the father.

The symbolism is clear—everyone is responsible for his own life and no one can be bothered with anyone else's problems. This moved Khrushchev to declare angrily, "Not even animals leave their children in the lurch, and in the picture, a Soviet man is doing just that!" But the picture will be shown shortly with only slight changes, and the concluding scene will be left intact.

This year much attention was drawn by two pictures on contemporary life, *I Walk Through Moscow* and *Man Follows the Sun*. In the latter, a special surprise is the excellent electronic avant-garde music by a young Kiev composer. Of course, the picture was criticized because of its music.

But the greatest acclaim by the public and the *younger* critics was given to the new version of *Hamlet* directed by the Leningrad director Kozintsev. In my opinion Hamlet's portrayal by the young actor Smoktunovsky was not inferior to that of Laurence Olivier. Smoktunovsky is considered an "actor-intellectual," and he leaves a memorable impression by employing hardly noticeable changes of shading in the timbre of his voice and the expression on his face. Where another actor would have performed in crescendo, Smoktunovsky creates a ghastly reality by minimal variations of tone and gesture. The music of Shostakovich is quite an experience. Ophelia was played by the daughter of the famous Russian poet and singer, Vertinsky, who in 1943 returned from exile with Stalin's personal approval.[12] Almost all the students with whom I spoke were enthusiastic about *Hamlet*. When Svetlana Sarukhanova, the Secretary of the Leningrad University Komsomol, who was showing me around Leningrad, learned that I had not seen the picture, she was shocked and insisted that I see it. She saw it three times. "This picture," she repeatedly told me, "is precisely about us, about youth, *da da!*"

Incidentally, while in Leningrad I had intended to visit the famous Cherkhasov—who played Ivan the Terrible and Aleksandr Nevsky in Eisenstein's pictures and received the 1964 Lenin Prize—but I only succeeded in talking to him by telephone. He was just about to leave for his *dacha,* and I was flying back to Moscow the next morning. He was preparing for the role of Karenin for the new film version of *Anna Karenina*.

New Western pictures are being shown in more than eighty Moscow movie theaters. *Divorce Italian Style* in twenty-nine theaters! *The Secrets of Paris, Fanfan the Tulip* starring Gerard Philipe, and many other films are also being shown. It was most difficult to get tickets for an American Western starring Yul Brynner, *The Magnificent Seven*. Also very popular are small satirical semi-

---

[12] Vertinsky was a well-known popular singer who emigrated to France and then, later, to the Far East. He accepted the invitation to return to Russia from Shanghai not in 1943 but in late 1945. Although his voice had long since failed him, Vertinsky was given a triumphant reception and allowed to give several concerts.

documentaries dealing with vital themes of contemporary life. Their title is *Wick* (of a candle) and they are regularly released and numbered.

THEATERS

Only about half of Moscow's thirty playhouses had regular programs in June. In the rest there were performances by provincial ensembles.

My friends, students at the Moscow Academy of Theater Art whom I had met at the Zagreb Festival of Student Theaters in 1963 (small world), are theater fanatics and were undoubtedly the best guides to the programs at the various capital theaters.

Unfortunately, they all agreed that the season had been very poor with few interesting new creations and only two or three performances worth seeing. Nevertheless, they insisted that first one must see any of the performances in the *Sovremennik* [the Contemporary Theater]. I managed somehow to get a ticket for Rostand's *Cyrano*. The play itself, in spite of excellent actors, would hardly have attracted much attention if not for the fact that the Contemporary Theater is trying to modernize the frozen tradition of the Russian stage (which has not changed a bit from the time of Krleža's *Excursion to Russia*) and break the long-standing gospel of Realism according to

Stanislavsky. It was the experimental aspects of the *Cyrano* production that had provoked the noisy enthusiasm of the public. The actors wore multicolored beards and hair (green, violet, red, orange); stage sets were hardly noticeable, only suggested and stylized; and the performance occasionally moved from the stage into the auditorium among the spectators.

The next day, at the Moscow Art Theater, I saw *I Walk Toward the Storm*, a drama in three acts by a very prolific but not very talented writer, Daniil Granin. This was one of the most popular items of last season, but it is simply incredible that the MKhAT people could have allowed such a stupid and dull play on their stage, and that the audience could watch it without booing. It was, of course, a so-called "production" play, of the type in which the main conflict between the heroes takes place in the struggle for construction, or for an invention, or for overfulfilling the norm. But while Dudintsev used the conflict between the engineer Lopatkin and the technical bureaucracy in his novel only as a means to express the deeper, existential tragedy of an heroic solitary man in a totalitarian society, the works of Granin, and of many others like him, hide only emptiness beneath a facade of artificially constructed and psychologically unmotivated conflict. The Art Theater people tried in vain to fill this emptiness. In fact, this probably explains why the director resorted to such effects as having some scenes take place on an airplane that is in flight on stage (scenic mastery indeed), booming thunderbolts and lightning flashes. It all resembles a very bad movie.

In the Moscow Satirical Theater I saw a comedy in two acts by Afanasy Salinsky, *A Lie for a Narrow Circle,* that had been much discussed in the Soviet press. This play was even called "the Soviet *Tartuffe*" by one critic. A woman, after learning that the man whom she was to marry has died as a hero on the front, declares that he was the father of her illegitimate daughter. Since this woman happens to be a high district official, she hopes to extract political profit from this. But a certain character emerges who claims to have proof that the deceased was not a hero but a traitor. The heroine is scared and denies her previous claim about the father of her daughter. The catastrophe arises when one of the positive personalities —an official of the State Archives and a former member of the NKVD (this is underlined in the play)—discovers the slanderer and saves the honor of the dead hero. All this is miserable, artificial, and the satire is soft: It does not lash out, it caresses.

My fourth performance, the drama *I Want To Believe* by I. Golosovsky, I saw in the Leningrad Theater and it seemed slightly more interesting. True, the plot is close to criminal-psychological mystery; it deals with the reputation of a woman accused of collaboration with the occupation forces during the War. But the basic idea of the play—that in spite of all possible facts and material proofs, feelings and intuition are always right—occasionally gave a psychological depth and strength to the dramatic conflict.

My most rewarding theater experience was certainly the play by S. Alyoshin, *The Hospital Ward,* which I saw in the Moscow Little Theater. This play was performed on forty-four stages in the Soviet Union in 1963, for a total of 1,320 performances, taking fourth place on the list of the most performed plays of the season.

The play takes place in a hospital, where four people lie in a ward and are occasionally visited by doctors or relatives. The number of characters in the play is small, but even among these few the weighty heritage of "Stalin's cult" lingers on. Two of the patients—the official Prozorov and the writer Novikov—get into an argument. There are no witnesses so they speak quite openly. After Novikov charges Prozorov with "officious superiority," Prozorov shows his real face:

Prozorov: And what Stalin said, you have already forgotten, naturally?

Novikov: Unfortunately, I remember it too well.

Prozorov: Ah, you are certainly one of those . . . Have you not been imprisoned?

Novikov: And who are you?

Prozorov: I am one of those who think that some should not have been released. Especially not the likes of you, the writers. They argue with you, they give advice, they persuade you, they spy on your opinions. And you let your tongues wag: You quarrel, discuss, push your opinions. We would have shown you in 1953. You would have been . . . (he gestures in the motion of turning a screw).

In this play, the Stalinist is depicted mercilessly as a disgusting person—so that he even cynically tells Novikov, who is about to undergo a difficult heart operation: "You will not get out of here. You will die under the knife. I have heard this in the dressing room. You will croak!" The play does not tell us whether Novikov survives the operation, but it shows Prozorov, cured, packing his luggage and going home. The success of this play demonstrates that the theater can be a vital force only when, as here, it takes an active part in solving the burning problems of man.

The theaters are often sold out even when they are presenting dull and stereotyped "production" plays. This is difficult to explain. In Yugoslavia, or in Western Europe, such plays would not attract an audience for a second performance—and rightly, I believe. Perhaps it is an invincible craving for life, for change, for something which is not the daily routine, that drives the Russians to the theater regardless of a play's quality. There is no other way to explain these packed theaters (and most of the Russian theaters offer two performances daily).

With rare exceptions, Soviet theaters today are museums. The popularity of the *Sovremennik* Theater, which is boldly introducing novelties (novelties only for the Soviet Union, that is), and is trying to rehabilitate Meyerhold and Tairov by means of stagecraft, shows that the Soviet theater will undoubtedly have to undergo a revolution.[13]

---

[13] Meyerhold has been the subject of several recent Soviet scholarly articles and was also featured in *Pages from Tarusa*. One important testing ground for stage productions in the style of Meyerhold in recent years which evidently did not come to the attention of Mihajlov: the various "children's theaters," often giving rise to the rather whimsical spectacle of juvenile plays with largely adult audiences.

Moscow students tried to put on Ionesco a few years ago, and today they are having a big success with Brecht, who is "too modern" for the Soviet professional theaters. I believe that in a few years the French avant-gardists will make a noisy entrance on the Soviet stage. They are badly needed to destroy all the stage museums. The resistance of "responsible" theatrical interests to any change is obvious: One manifestation of this is the conscious neglect of Evgeny Shvarts, undoubtedly the greatest modern Russian dramatist. Shvarts is not officially in disfavor and productions of his satirical plays have enjoyed memorable successes in the Soviet Union and abroad (his play *Dragon* was enthusiastically received in New York last season), but the theater administrators are reluctant to include his plays in their repertories. I therefore could not see any of them performed in Moscow or Leningrad.

Shvarts, born in 1896, was known for many years as a writer of brilliant children's plays. Not until after he died did the public learn that Shvarts was also an ingenious satirist, and that he had written during the darkness of the "cult" some of the most significant satirical plays of 20th century Russia.

In 1940, on the eve of Russia's entry into World War II and at the time of the dreadful purges and inhuman "lacquering" in the arts, Shvarts wrote his best play, *The Shadow*. Here the great artist gaily laughed at life and ridiculed all that was sinister and dreadful in his country, although revealing unlimited faith that in the end justice would triumph. Naturally, the play was kept in a drawer for years, while plays by the "official satirist" Boris Romashov, a "lacquerizer," were performed on Russian stages (*It May Happen to Anybody* in 1941, etc.).

The plot of *The Shadow* is simple and is based on a well-known Andersen tale. A strange Scholar comes to an exotic kingdom, falls in love with the Princess, then loses his Shadow, which returns to steal the Princess from the Scholar and become the ruler. The Shadow, personifying all the sinister and wicked traits of human nature, and aided by courtiers, tries to break the will of the Scholar and force him into subservience. The Scholar chooses death instead, and when his head is chopped off the Shadow's head falls off at the same time.

The courtiers, in order to revive the Shadow, bring the Scholar back to life by using "magic water." The basic idea is that bureaucracy has taken the head off the Revolution, but it will not be able to survive itself unless it revives the Revolution.

The value of this play does not lie in the borrowed plot. Its originality and its inimitable artistic magic are due to a strange mixture of tender poetry and penetrating satire. Through a confused tangle of conflicts and brilliant, witty dialogue (the grotesque form is similar to the works of Ionesco and the French avant-garde writers) all the characters from the time of the "personality cult" are exposed: secret ministers and secret police, spies and informers, intriguers and careerists, corrupt journalists and artists—all those, as Shvarts says, "who worked as honorary assessor-cannibals in municipal pawn shops of live people."

Interestingly, Shvarts identifies the bureaucrats with the capitalist class. The only thing they wish, as the Shadow says, is that there will never be "any changes, any plans, any day-dreaming." The officials are invincible because they are indifferent to everything: to life, to death, to great discoveries. Allusions to real events occur often throughout the play. Speaking of the Princess' father, the King, one person observes:

"The deceased was a clever man, but serving a King can spoil one's nature. At the very beginning of his rule, the Prime Minister, whom the King trusted more than his own father, poisoned the King's sister. The King executed the Prime Minister. Another Prime Minister was not a poisoner, but he lied so much to the King that the King did not trust anybody, not even himself. The third Prime Minister was not a liar, but he was terribly sly. He shuffled and shuffled and knit the finest web around even the simplest matters. While listening to his last report, the King wanted to say: 'I confirm it.' But he suddenly buzzed instead, in a high-pitched tone like a fly entangled in a cobweb, and the Minister was dismissed at the request of the King's physician. The fourth Prime Minister was not sly. He was frank and simple. He stole the King's golden cigaret case and ran away. So the King abandoned administrative affairs. From then on the Prime Ministers started replacing each other, while the King took up the theater. However, people say this is an even more difficult task than running a state."

Shvarts exposes not only bureaucracy, but also those who make its existence possible. These are, as one character in the play says, "The circle of right people." "Oh, we are actors, writers, courtiers. Even a Minister comes occasionally. We are not elegant, nor devoid of prejudices, but we understand everything."

In spite of all this, the evil forces are conquered. Because, as the Scholar says: "Life is on one side, the Shadow on the other. All my knowledge tells me that the Shadow may win only for a certain time. The world depends on us, on people who create. But in order to win, one should even risk death."

The Shadow is a truly important work.[14] Modern dramatic technique (so scarce in contemporary Russian dramatic literature), powerful language, countless scenic effects which come to life only on the stage and cannot be expressed on paper—all these qualities make the play a masterpiece comparable to plays by the best of Soviet playwrights: Nikolai Pogodin, Vsevolod Vishnevsky, Vsevolod Ivanov and Leonov.

The Scholar says at one point in the play: "Your country, alas! resembles all the countries of the world. Richness and poverty, aristocracy and slavery, death and happiness, reason and stupidity, innocence, crime, conscience, shamelessness—they are so thickly mixed that one is simply terrified. It will be very difficult to disentangle it all, to separate it and bring it back into order, so that nothing living gets hurt." At the time *The Shadow*

[14] *The Shadow* is available in translation in the paperback *An Anthology of Russian Plays*, Vol. 2 (Vintage).

was written, of course, even such a "heretical" thought would have been sufficient for the play to be proscribed. And this is exactly what happened, for a while. But whatever the sinister forces and shadows of all kinds may do, life still triumphs. The experience of the Prime Minister in the play is certainly relevant when he says: "During the long years of my service I discovered a not very pleasant law. At the very moment when we are finally winning, life suddenly raises its head." His collaborator replies: "It raises its head? . . . Did you call for the royal headsman?!" But it is too late.

Today a lot is being written on Shvarts in the Soviet magazines. *Znamya* (No. 5, 1964), for example, contained interesting memoirs of the Soviet playwright Aleksandr Stein (born in 1906), entitled "How Plots Are Born," in which he describes his encounters with Boris Lavrenyov, with the émigré poet Vertinsky, with Shvarts and others. Stein writes: "Most of Evgeny Shvarts' plays were produced and published after his death. He was only recognized as an artist, and evaluated with booming praise in articles and books, after his death." (*The Shadow* first saw the light of day in 1956.) Of another of Shvarts' important plays, *The Naked King*, written in 1934, Stein wrote: "They staged *The Naked King* only in 1960 in the *Sovremennik* Theater, which was founded as a result of the enthusiasm of the MKhAT students, and even more so, as a result of the spirit of the new times."

During the War Evgeny Shvarts and his wife, in spite

of his serious heart illness, refused to be evacuated from Leningrad. They endured all the sufferings of the three-year siege. "In 1946," Stein wrote, "I met Evgeny Shvarts, very depressed and lost. . . . He was returning from a conference at which Akhmatova and Zoshchenko were expelled from the Writers' Union, and in their absence at that. Zoshchenko was called rabble, and Akhmatova a prostitute."[15] From Stein's memoirs there emerges a portrait of Shvarts as a talented playwright and an exceptionally honest and humane man, undeservedly ignored for too many years. The significance of Shvarts for the future of Russian drama is enormous.

LEONID LEONOV

The main street in Moscow, Gorky Street, is called "The Moscow Broadway" by the students. The street is wide and has underground passages. At one end it enters Red Square in front of the Kremlin; at the other, it continues into Leningrad Lane leading to the famous Volokolamsky Road. This was where those famous battles were fought

---

[15] More specifically, Anna Akhmatova—today Russia's greatest living poet—was accused by Soviet cultural commissar Andrei Zhdanov in August, 1946 of being "a cross between a nun and a whore" who "poisons the minds of our young people." Subsequently she was imprisoned for seventeen months.

in 1941, when this artery leading toward the Kremlin was penetrated by Guderian's tanks.

On almost every house in Gorky Street there is a memorial plaque: Here, at such and such time, lived and worked Demyan Bedny, or Fadeev, or Nikolai Ostrovsky, Paval Korchagin's creator. Or here, on this or that day in 1918 or 1919 or 1922, Lenin made a speech. At the very beginning of the street, not far from Red Square, is Ilya Ehrenburg's home, and at the end, Leonid Leonov's. These two famous veterans—from the times when Esenin used to carouse in inns, Lenin made speeches, and Dzherzhinsky was arresting the "contras" in Moscow—had probably even then chosen the houses on which memorial plaques would some day hang.

It is a strange feeling to see with your own eyes and talk to people who already belonged to history before you were born. One unwillingly doubts that the authors of books one read in school as classics still exist in reality —that they eat, drink, smoke, read newspapers. It is as if a statue descended from its pedestal and started an ordinary, everyday conversation.

I had such a feeling of unreality while approaching 54 Gorky Street, where the author of *The Thief, The Badgers,* and *Russian Forest* lives in an apartment on the seventh floor. A tall, gray-haired man with thick glasses and a nervous look opened the door for me and took me to his study. After two hours of talk, I had to admit to myself that I was deeply disappointed. Leonov is not an interesting man to speak to (which only confirmed the fact that great writers are often dull people in real life, and vice versa).

Leonov is rewriting most of his earlier works. The new version of *The Thief* has already provoked debate. He told me that Stalin personally crossed out with red pencil many parts of the first draft of his novel. "Now I can write freely, that's why I am rewriting my old works," he said.

The new version of Leonov's play *Invasion* is finished. The hero—in the first version condemned to prison for murdering the woman he loved—has been replaced by a political offender, a former camp prisoner. The well-known play *Golden Carriage* has also been rewritten.

"I suffer from Gogol's illness," Leonov told me, "nothing I write can satisfy me." He said that he works "terribly much, even on the First of May." He has not read Kafka's *The Trial;* he has a negative attitude toward modern art. "How would it look if while speaking to you I put my glasses on my mouth, and not on my nose?" he said, ridiculing modern painting. When I started to defend modernism, trying to explain that Picasso was precisely the same type of realist as Rembrandt, but the subject of his realism was different—the inner world, the reality of the alienated man—Leonov got so angry that he exclaimed: "One should fight against this even with a sword!" He attacked passionately a jazz version of "Ave Maria." (It seems that this composition gave him unusual pain. I had already read one of his attacks on it in our press.) When I told him that he himself was, from a stylistic point of view, a pupil of the "Russian Kafka," Aleksei Remizov, he retorted that he had not read a single page of Remizov's works. This seems very unlikely, and frankly I don't believe him, considering that Remizov was at the peak of his popularity in Russia at the very time that Leonov started to write. Moreover, the magazine *Russkoe Iskusstvo* (*Russian Art*, No. 1, 1923) carried an essay by Evgeny Zamyatin, entitled "New Russian Prose," in which Zamyatin wrote: "Leonov is undoubtedly a literary son of Remizov; that is why his language is crimson, elastic, very Russian, but without any slang." In our talk Leonov spoke with enthusiasm about Yugoslavia. "Whenever I pass by the Yugoslav Embassy, I say to myself—my brother lives here." He added, "The Yugoslavs have a literary intelligentsia."

Leonov had no solutions to the problems of contemporary humanity. He is most concerned with the rapid growth of the earth's population. "Where is this leading us?" he asks, pointing out that not even the wars we went through had much diminished the population. Concerning the situation in the Soviet Union, Leonov feels the essential and only important problem today is to discover and remove the causes that have made Stalinism possible. Unfortunately, he complained, the authorities are still slowing down liberalization by all possible means. "About the Soviet concentration camps," Leonov said, "people will be writing for the next eighty years."

Part II

CONCENTRATION CAMP THEMES

Leonov is right. The Soviet concentration camp theme has only begun to appear in Russian literature. A year ago Khrushchev reported that literary magazines had received about 10,000 novels, short stories and memoirs on the camp theme—which is not so much, considering that during the three decades of the Stalin era eight to twelve million people were deported to the camps. Of the 10,000 manuscripts, only a small number were published. ("One should be very careful with this," Khrushchev said.) Still, Soviet magazines are beginning to look like annals of the crimes of Philip II's Inquisition. The majority of the prisoners who were lucky enough to survive until 1956–57 and get out of the camps do not want to keep silent. Thus today the Soviet authorities are faced with two alternatives: to send former prisoners back to the camps (which the Kremlin neither wants to do nor could do any more), or to let them talk. The latter is happening, and the brakes are weakening.

Next to the novel *One Day in the Life of Ivan Denisovich* by Aleksandr Solzhenitsyn, the greatest interest has been stirred by the memoirs of General of the Army A. V. Gorbatov, published in *Novy Mir* (Nos. 3, 4, 5, 1964). The most moving parts of these memoirs are those where Gorbatov describes the Soviet prisons and camps in which he was held before World War II, a victim of false denunciations. Especially interesting is the fact that he names his torturers who, to this day, have not been punished:

"Soon they started calling me to interrogations again. This time there were five of them. During one of these interrogations, I learned by chance that the name of my investigator-beast was Stolbunsky. I don't know where he is now. If he is alive, I would like him to read these lines and to feel all my contempt for him—not only the contempt I have now, but that I had then when I was in his hands. However, I believe that he was well aware of this. In addition to the investigator, two strapping executioners took part in the interrogations. I still hear—just as when they were carrying me away, exhausted and covered with blood—the ominous, screaming voice of Stolbunsky: 'You will sign, you will sign!' I endured this torture also during the second cycle of interrogations. When they started the third cycle, however, I wanted to die as quickly as possible."

Gorbatov also gives revealing descriptions of the camp regime, and of the distinction the authorities made between common criminals and "enemies of the people": "The guards, headed by their chief, got on very well with the criminals, encouraging their inclination toward violence and using them to ridicule the 'enemies of the people' . . . As a rule, they assigned the 'enemies of the people' to more difficult tasks, while the 'friends,' i.e., the criminals, got the lighter jobs." About the actual "work," he writes: "It will be very difficult for readers to imagine this picture. On the slopes of hills, in a line nearly two and a half miles long, exhausted people—not people, but shadows—drag along, stretching out their necks like cranes flying, straining their last bit of energy hauling wood. It is hard to pull wood down a hill, it is more difficult on a plain, but up even the slightest slope it becomes simply impossible. People stumble, fall down, get up, and fall down again. The load moves forward only when someone from the rear comes to help." And about the women's camps Gorbatov writes: ". . . But these were our mothers, wives, sisters, daughters, most of them condemned because they were family members of the 'enemies of the people.' If we had not committed any offense, we were at least accused of something, while these wretched women were simply victims of a cruel and blatant despotism."

Such an open disclosure of truth about the crimes of the Stalin years and the tragedy of the Soviet people poses a problem that is still being evaded: Those people who actively fought against Stalinism long before 1956, and who revealed the truth about conditions in the Soviet Union, are still considered criminals and "traitors," although all that they wrote at the time about the USSR could be published today in Soviet magazines. There is, for example, the well-known case of Ivan Solonevich, who in 1937 escaped to the West from a camp in Siberia and then wrote a widely read book, *Russia in a Concentration Camp*. The book is similar to Gorbatov's memoirs and to other Soviet works on the camps. But Ivan Solonevich is still considered a "traitor to the working people, capitalist hireling," and so on.

And so in the USSR today there is an ambiguous official attitude toward Stalinism and toward the early anti-Stalinists. On the one hand, Stalin is condemned as tyrannical and criminal, while on the other, anti-Stalinists are condemned in the same manner. Sooner or later such an abnormal situation will have to be resolved, and since nowadays the official anti-Stalinist forces are leading a mighty offensive, it seems that the problem will come to the agenda sooner rather than later.

Many who were imprisoned remain to be cleared, for rehabilitations have only just begun. An MGU student told me: "They have rehabilitated only their own people. The thousands of honest people—the non-members of the Party—what has happened to them?" And many people whom I met spoke with sarcasm about the procedure for rehabilitation of those who died in prisons or camps. The family receives a form on which the name of the prisoner and the official confirmation of the rehabilitation is written—and that is all. There is nothing about when, where or how the "rehabilitated" dead lost their lives, and there is no way of finding this out. Since there are few families that do not have at least one member to be "rehabilitated," discontent about half-way liquidation of Stalinism is widespread. At the same time, everybody feels strongly that the fight against Stalinism has only started, and people are optimistic regarding the eventual outcome of this fight.

The Soviet press is writing less and less about Fascist and Nazi camps, to avoid any comparisons with the Soviet camps. This is quite understandable. The first "death camps" were not founded by the Germans, but by the Soviets. In 1921, near Arkhanghelsk, they set up Kholmogor camp, for the sole purpose of physically destroying the prisoners. It operated successfully for many years and swallowed up many of the Bolsheviks' former allies—members of the non-Bolshevik revolutionary parties (S-Rs, Mensheviks and others). Ivan Shmelyov, the émigré writer who has recently been rehabilitated in the Soviet Union, describes in his famous book, *Dead Men's Sun* (to which Thomas Mann wrote an introduction), the dreadful years after the Russian civil war when in 1920–21 alone 120,000 men and women in the Crimea were shot without trial. Stories are still being told about a certain Vera Grebenykova, a young woman known pseudonymously as "Dora," who "worked" at that time in Odessa. She personally tortured and killed 700 prisoners.

Even in the matter of genocide Hitler had been anticipated. On the eve of World War II numerous peoples in the regions along the Turkish-Iranian border were deported to Northern Siberia where, unaccustomed to the cold climate, they died like flies. It is not surprising that so many Red Army units consisting of Kalmuks, Tartars, Circassians and other minor nationalities subjected to Kremlin repression, deserted to the side of Hitler's criminals.

The same reasons caused massive defections by the Don Cossacks. The emergence of the anti-Soviet Cossack army of Lieutenant General Andrei A. Vlassov—the so-called Russian Liberation Army—represents a unique phenomenon in the history of the Russian people. For more than three hundred years the Cossacks had been the solid foundation of the Russian state and the best guarantee against any enemy. The magazine *Yunost* recently published Evgeny Pilyar's novel *Man Remains Man*, in which he initiates a discussion of the extremely sensitive problem of Soviet attitudes toward the Cossacks. Pilyar describes the bravery of the Cossacks during beating they received at the hands of Red Army interrogators after being captured. He finds himself in a dilemma, and he leaves this question unanswered: "Yes, I know they are traitors, but how can one explain treason committed by such people—ordinary Russian peasants—who go to their death now so fearlessly?"

There is also the related problem of the partisan movements in occupied territory that fought the Germans and the Red Army simultaneously, representing a so-called "third force." Very soon, undoubtedly, the whole historical view of World War II will have to be subjected to thorough revision. In the case of Stalin's activity in the Army, this has already started.

The magazine *Znamya* (No. 5, 1964) published the final chapters of Konstantin Simonov's novel, *Soldiers Are Not Born* (the earlier installments appeared in Nos. 8–11, 1963, and 1–4, 1964). Highly praised by the Soviet press, its theme is the War and the events leading up to it. Of particular interest in Simonov's description of Stalin's inner world, of his thoughts and feelings. While the "father of the people" had been depicted in the best possible light in literary works prior to 1956, this is the first Soviet literary work which tries to present him realistically. The hero of the novel, General Serpilin, has a meeting with Stalin in the Kremlin and at one point is tempted to ask him to explain the true purpose of the purges in the Army, whose victims were to include himself:

"Then Stalin turned and walked back facing him, and for a moment Serpilin remembered that face as it had appeared in May 1937, at the final ceremony at the Academy. His face was as calm then as now, and within a week Tukhachevsky and Yakir were arrested, Gamarnik committed suicide, and it had started, started . . . !

"At the beginning, after the first secret military trial, he was horrified and believed a plot had really existed. He could not have doubted it: What else but a horrible, ambitious plot, detected at the last moment, could have sent to death these men who just a month earlier were looked upon as the flower of the Army? Only later, when he himself was confronted with the senseless and monstrous accusations that were being thrown at men who could not even dream why they were being accused, only then the thought started to torture him: Maybe the same thing that was happening to him now had happened to those at the beginning, and would happen with others.

"He watched Stalin approach him and thought, I will say: 'Comrade Stalin, explain all this to me. Confide. Everything from the very beginning, right from the very beginning!' Stalin approached, sat down and bent forward to clean his pipe over the ashtray. Serpilin, who in a surge of feeling was prepared to tell him all this, suddenly saw, close up, Stalin's mercilessly calm eyes, occupied by some distant and cruel thought, maybe provoked by the memory of Yezhov. He saw these eyes and suddenly realized what he had always feared even to consider: There is nobody to complain to!"

Nevertheless, Simonov has Serpilin remaining loyal to Stalin. Simonov offers this explanation of why not a single serious plot was organized against the dictator: "Yes, Serpilin would have protected him with his own body, not only because it was his duty as a soldier, but because of his conviction that Stalin's death would be a disaster for the country in wartime, with endless consequences. With hatred he thought of the Germans, of how they would rejoice in Stalin's death . . ."

Simonov characterizes "the wise leader" Stalin as a man who fears people—a tiny, vain, vindictive, treacherous, unbalanced man. "Not only now, but also at that time [of the Revolution] he did not like to go among the soldiers, and in the bottom of his heart he feared people who were not at a sufficient distance from him. . . . With all this inhuman contempt for people, he still had not lost so human a trait as the ability to feel offended by them." Simonov tells of one occasion when Stalin nominated a division commander for the post of Army commander. At the very moment when the general was to take over his new command, Stalin changed his mind, and the unfortunate man was shot.

Prewar purges weakened the country and the Army to such an extent, Simonov writes, that Stalin must bear the blame for the great Russian defeats in the first phases of War. Talking with a friend, General Serpilin learns about an inspection of 225 regiment commanders in 1941; " 'And of these 225, how many do you think had graduated from ordinary military schools? Twenty-five; And the other 200—only courses for second lieutenants and regimental schools. . . . And the Germans?' said Ivan Aleksevich, his voice trembling when he saw those tears on Serpilin's usually composed face. 'And the Germans— of all the regimental commanders, both prisoners and dead, from whom we have taken documents during one and a half years, I have not see a single case of a regimental commander not having had experience as an officer in the First World War. . . . War is right in front of our nose, and of 225 regimental commanders, not a single one has graduated from the Academy.' "

The truth about forced collectivization, executed at the price of about eight million Russian peasant lives, has also begun to be revealed in a major way—in the second part of Sholokhov's *Virgin Land Upturned*, published in 1959–60 in the magazine *Zvezda* [*Star*], and more openly in 1962 in the novel by M. Zestev, *Tatyana Tarkhanova*. The novel describes the deportation one night of a great number of peasants from the village of Pukhlyaky who had been classified as kulaks. Among the deportees is the novel's hero, Ignat Tarkhanov, an honest man who had never exploited anyone else's labor, who had never committed an offense, and who possessed some modest property on which he and his wife labored peacefully and diligently. They had a house, a horse, a cow and a piece of land. The violence against them and other kulaks is described as being so monstrous that even the local Communists who were directing the night's operation against their neighbors began to doubt the correctness of the measure. One of the Communists thinks: "It might have been quite sufficient if only a dozen or so of the rich people were deported." In Moscow I heard the slogan popular among the Soviet *kolkhozniks* (collective farmers): "Lenin gave us the land—Stalin took it away."

At the now famous meeting of Party representatives and writers on March 8, 1963, Khrushchev read a letter that Mikhail Sholokhov had sent to Stalin (April 16, 1933) in defense of the peasants of his region:

"If what I described deserves the attention of the Central Committee," wrote Sholokhov to Stalin, "do send to the Veshen region real Communists who would have the courage, regardless of anybody, to unmask all those who are responsible for ruining the *kolkhoz* economy of the region—people who would indeed investigate and expose not only all those who used disgusting methods of torturing, beating and ridiculing the *kolkhozniks*, but also those who inspired them in this work."[16] Of course, Stalin did not react because he himself was the main source of inspiration for the "methods," although he hypocritically "undertook to defend" the peasants in his well-known article entitled "Dizziness from Success."

---

[16] The reference is to a letter from Sholokhov to Stalin cited by Khrushchev in a speech to show that there was resistance voiced against "arbitrary rule" under Stalin. (*Pravda,* March 10, 1963.)

LABOR CAMP FOLKLORE

One evening I found myself at a lively student party in the MGU dormitory. People were singing some of the composer-singer Bulat Okudzhava's songs, drinking and playing guitars. It was a night I shall remember all my life. The group was joined by a young Siberian, an excellent guitarist and singer popular with the MGU students. Without much urging, he started to sing, accompanying himself on the guitar, in an untrained yet excellent baritone. The party joined him in the refrains. But what moved me most were the songs themselves—I never supposed that songs like these existed in the USSR. They were camp prisoners' songs of all varieties: comic, full of despair, and cynical. It was Russia speaking through them, the Russia we know from Tolstoy and Dostoevsky. They were true folk melodies, not stylized like the ones we hear on the Soviet radio, but raw, sometimes naïve, always deep, genuinely melodic, and tragic.

These songs were born in the depths of the Siberian wilderness, around campfires in the woods, where the numerous prisoners, exhausted from a hard day's work, miserable food and beatings, warmed themselves. There is a painful irony and cynicism in these songs—in no small part because the prisoners were forced to listen daily to Government broadcasts blaring out that the USSR was the first country of Socialism, the most righteous fatherland of all working people, the freest country in the world. And the broadcasts were accompanied by a song that the Soviet radio played over and over each day, *Large Is My Fatherland*, which included the following verses:

From Moscow to the borders,
From the Southern woods to the Northern seas,
You pace the land like the Lord
Of your immense fatherland.
At our table no one is unwelcome,
Everyone is rewarded according to his merits.
We are writing down in golden letters
The national Stalin law.

The camp responded to Stalin with its own song:

Comrade Stalin, you are a great scientist,
In linguistics you have learned the very essence,
While I am an ordinary Soviet prisoner
And my only friend is the grey wolf of Bryansk.

In my conscience, I don't know why I am imprisoned,
But the prosecutors are obviously right,
And here I am in the Turukhansk country
Where you were slaving during the time of Tsar.[17]

Here I am in the Turukhansk country,
Where the guards are severe and rude.
But, of course, I understand all this
As the culmination of the class struggle.

We silently confessed someone else's sins,
Step by step we marched to meet the evil destiny,

[17] Stalin was a prisoner in a camp near Turukhansk in Siberia, from 1913–1917.

We believed you so much, Comrade Stalin,
As we perhaps did not believe ourselves.

With rain, or snow, or mosquitoes around us,
We are in the wilderness from dawn to dawn.
You made the flame from "Iskra" here,
Thank you. I warm myself beside the fire.[18]

I see you in your Party cap
And military cloak as you go to the parade.
We are cutting wood while the Stalinist splinters
Continue to fly in all directions.

Your chest is full of decorations and medals,
And your hair turned grey from worries.
Six times you escaped from prison,
While I, a fool, didn't make it once.

Yesterday we buried two Marxists,
We didn't cover them with flags;
One of them had "the Rightist deviation"
And the other, as it turned out, not even this.

But before he closed his eyes forever,
He left you his tobacco pouch and his last words.
He begged you to clear all this up
And softly exclaimed, "Stalin is a brain!"

Live for a hundred years, Comrade Stalin!
And even if I have to die here,

[18] *Iskra* (spark) was a pre-1917 revolutionary newspaper published in Geneva to which Lenin among others contributed.

May the percentage of production of steel
Keep increasing per capita.

There is a moving song about Magadan, in the center of the Kolima peninsula, which was jammed with concentration camps. The song ends:

Be cursed, Kolima,
Land of paradise, as they called you.
You will forget me
For there is no return from here.

I know you are not expecting me,
And you don't read my letters;
You are not coming to meet me,
And if you come, you will not recognize me.

Despair is expressed in incredibly tragic melodies. The Siberian singer announced one, *A Song from a Place Not So Far Away:*

You wake up early, and the town is still sleeping.
The prison does not sleep, it has watched all night.
The heart aches dully
As if the flame had touched it.

And if you say a word in the line
You are pulled out as if by tongs
And tomorrow, expect for sure
To be thrown into cold solitary with your things.

If you say a word, you are cursed,
But one quickly gets used to curses,

And by habit you put your hands at your back,
Your grim eyes lowered toward the ground.

There are innumerable prison songs. One bitter song begins:

They finished me, the bastards, they finished me
They destroyed my youth,
My golden hair has turned white,
And I am on the edge of ruin.[19]

But there are a lot of comic songs too. A popular one is *Anna Karenina,* which tells how the heroine of the novel lived in Moscow as an aristocrat and idler, suffering from "Russian love," and how she involved herself with Vronsky, an officer and a "terrible rascal" because he was a product of pre-Soviet society. When Vronsky "forgot his promise and showed that he was ideologically backward," Anna "proudly lay down on the train tracks, and nobody, in those long lost days of capitalism, thought to save her."

Thus the foolish conquettes died,
Whom the Tsarist regime has fed,
But we, who lived through the days of "semiletka,"[20]
We don't sympathize with them.

---

[19] It has been pointed out that some of the songs cited by Mihajlov originated long before the Soviet concentration camps were set up, which does not, however, alter the fact that they became, subsequently, Soviet concentration camp songs. As Mihajlov notes later, no research in this important area of folklore has been permitted by the Soviets.

[20] "*Semiletka*" is the gruffly affectionate diminutive for the standard seven-year labor sentence.

The song ends with verses which reveal that the singer is, in fact, Sergei, the son of Anna Karenina, who begs the listeners to give him "at least a piece of bread," so that he can finish his life differently from his mother.

Another song, *Of the Factory, Of the Union,* is full of original folk humor:

> *Seryozha the proletarian worked in the factory,*
> *He was a completely aware Marxist*
> *And he was a member of Profkom*
> *And he was a member of Mestkom*
> *All in all, a 100 per cent activist.*

The song tells us how his girl friend Manka suffered from "ideological deviation"; she wore short skirts and used lipstick. Seryozha tells her to stop, not to compromise him, and calls her a "harmful beast whom one must fight." Manka tells him to go to hell, but Seryozha won't give up, and he continues to fight with her.

Some songs reveal a persistent spirit of creativity. This *Easter* song was probably written after 1956:

> *I watch the sky with an enlightened look,*
> *Already in the morning I realize what the matter is,*
> *I like this Easter day as much as "the Day of Miners,"*
> *As much as the "Anniversary of Our Army."*
>
> *Today the eggs are being broken with a crunch*
> *And the ringing of bells thrills the ear.*
> *The proletarians of all countries are uniting,*
> *Around the laid-out Easter table.*

Everybody dyes eggs blue and green,
But I dye them only red,
And I carry them proudly, like flags,
Like symbols of our heroic victories.

Accompanied by the solemn ringing of knives and
spoons
The smell of the Easter cake went to our noses.
How nice it is in this forest of bottles
To see the face even of the informer.

Let's kiss each other, passerby,
Forgive me my pure joy,
We are beginning to look like human beings,
Let's say it again, Christ is risen!

A truly moving song from the postwar years tells of the sorrow of a wounded soldier, whose wife sleeps with a military clerk who has been awarded many medals:

I was the scout for the battalion
And he—a headquarters clerk.
I was responsible for Russia,
And he was sleeping with my wife.

O my wife, my wretched Klanka,
Is it really all the same to you—
That you exchanged, poor fool,
An eagle for such offal?

An eagle and a marvel of a man,
I wouldn't stoop to talk to him.

On the way from Moscow to Berlin
I walked over corpses for three years.

I walked, and later in the hospital
I lay in the embrace of death;
And the nurses were crying,
And the scalpel in the surgeon's hand trembled.

And my neighbor, a hero, was crying.
Colonel and three times a hero,
Wiping his tears with his sleeve,
With his feverish, soldierly arm.

The cursed piece of iron
Got my bladder
I reached down for my artificial limb from under the
*   bed.*
And there was the clerk from headquarters.

I bashed him on his white chest,
I tore off his medals.
Look on, men of Russia,
My native country.

I madly adored
My wretched Klanka!
But my artificial limb did not get erected for her
So I beat her black and blue with my crutch.

I was surprised by a song about Patrice Lumumba, obviously written quite recently:

Patrice Lumumba was killed far away from us
And the Congo became poorer without him.

His wife, beautiful Pauline,
Refused to live with another man.

There was a meeting in the Factory of Litsnachov
And in the Factory of the Red Proletarian as well:
Curse you, Tshombe, Lumumba's executioner,
Curse you, Mobuto with the black snout.

Beggars' songs, soldiers' songs, prisoners' songs: Russia is rich with tears and beauty. How many songs are still unknown to the public because men have only recently dared begin singing them openly? The students, as usual, are the first to do it. Is anybody writing them down, or are they going to be written down only when the things they are singing about have become remote and uninteresting history? I had the rare luck, quite by chance, to be probably the first foreigner to record about 20 of these songs on tape, with the help of the students. I brought the tapes back to Yugoslavia with me. These songs are undoubtedly the most significant new folklore of our time, and it is understandable why it has originated in Russia. The concentration camps were a natural breeding ground for such folk music—the only possible form of creation under camp conditions. These songs, from the moment they are officially sanctioned, will surely be sung, for a whole century, as the convicts' songs of the last century are sung today, though they are surpassed in beauty by this new music of the people.

What are the numerous Soviet folklore institutes doing? Thank you, my Siberian friend, and all my other distant friends in Moscow. The songs of the Russian people will be heard, regardless of whether they are written about in the USSR or silently ignored.

BELLA AKHMADULINA

One Sunday shortly before I left Moscow, together with my official guide Oleg Merkurov, I went to the *dacha* of the most popular young Russian poetess—Bella Akhmadulina. Her *dacha* is in the settlement of Vatutino, about twenty-two miles from Moscow, in a beautiful, dense forest. She lives there all year long with her husband, the writer Yury Nagibin, and comes to Moscow only on business. This is how many wealthy Muscovites live. After dusty, noisy Moscow, Vatutino is truly a green paradise, all silence and forest. In spite of the fact that on the telephone the poetess had given us detailed traveling instructions, we wandered quite a while through "forest streets," where the *dachas* can hardly be seen through the trees, before finding Akhmadulina's.

The comfortably furnished house was fitted with paintings and sculpture by young Russian artists whose works still could not be seen in any public place. The lovely and spoiled young lady with the Tartar features, wearing slacks and sport shirt, a cigaret between her lips, received us graciously. A completely un-Soviet impression—which explains why it is her picture that most often appears on the covers of European and American magazines. They say that half of Moscow's students are in love with Akhmadulina.

The hostess offered us American cigarets (they are "chic" in Moscow), and in an animated conversation that lasted for an hour she told me so much about herself that I could now easily write her biography. But that will be done by someone else, and I will set down here only a few of the details that particularly struck me.

Like other poets, Akhmadulina considers Pasternak, Mandelstam and Tsvetaeva as her teachers. Andrei Voznesensky, her close friend, asked her several times to visit Pasternak, whom she had always admired: Akhmadulina refused for fear of being disappointed by him, she explained. She also avoided meeting Anna Akhmatova, but eventually met her by accident, and once even drove her on an excursion. The car broke down, and Akhmatova had to return home by taxi. The car has been a source of trouble for them in other ways, too. Because of a traffic violation, Bella's driver's license was taken away. Her husband cursed—and his driver's license was also taken away. They travel to Moscow by bus now.

While we were sitting on the terrace and talking, two neighbors dropped in. When we were introduced I did not pay close attention to their names. The older bald man told a fascinating story about the word *balagan* (fair), and its journey through history and through different languages. The word derives from the Arabic and can be found, somewhat transformed, in Russian, Spanish and other European languages, so that it is difficult to discover its root.[21] "A word that met its own reflection and could not recognize itself," he said. I asked the man if he was a linguist. He looked at me with surprise, and said with a smile: "Yes, of course I am." Only after their departure did I learn that my "linguist" was, in fact, the famous poet Pavel Antokolsky.

Later Bella recited (and extremely well) fragments of her newest and thus her favorite work, *The Poem About Rain*. To judge from this poem, it seems that Russian poetry is moving toward the modernism of Khlebnikov, Bely, early Mayakovsky and Pasternak. In the poem, rain enters a home, plays with children, and behaves as a living creature. There is not a trace of Socialist Realism. Akhmadulina is clearly a very talented and strong poetic personality. Several years ago I read one of her collections of poems and was deeply disappointed; I feel differently now. *The Poem about Rain* and *The Poem about Pasternak* (printed in *Literaturnaya Gruziya* [*Literary Georgia*]) show an original talent which, in the collection I had read, has been smothered with "official" subjects.

But Akhmadulina, like Bulat Okudzhava, is writing more and more prose these days. She would like to write in the style of Proust, whom she admires and reads in Russian translation (she owns the first and only 1929

---

[21] The word's roots denote an open place or platform at a fair where performances were given. Some linguists consider that the English "balcony" is derived from the same source.

edition of *Remembrance of Things Past,* in four volumes, with a preface by Lunacharsky—a rare set today).

"Like Proust," Akhmadulina is writing a rather long story, *Pushkin's Country,* but admits that this kind of prose is still not welcome. Her short story "Little Old Woman" could not be printed: it was termed "decadent." She had heard of Joyce, but not of Virginia Woolf. Before our departure we learned that many other writers live in Vatutino: Tendryakov, Bondaryov, Tvardovsky. We decided to visit them. Bondaryov was closest.

BONDARYOV

Akhmadulina took us to Bondaryov's *dacha.* He is one of the most famous young Russian writers. He was born in 1924. From school he went directly to war, and when he returned to civilian life, he refused—like most of the heroes in his books—to compromise with his conscience: Out of the blue, he had to develop a critical stance toward existing conditions. Though he has published books since 1953 (a collection of short stories, *On the Big River,* 1953; and the novels *Youth of the Commandant,* 1956; *Battalions Seek Artillery Fire,* 1958; *The Last Salvos,* 1959), he first gained wide popularity only with the publication of his novel *Tishina* (*Silence,* 1962). This describes the tribulations of students during the "cult" era, the imprisoning of innocent men charged with being "Trotskyites," the persecution of "cosmopolitanism" in art, etc. Konstantin Paustovsky called this novel a "work of great courage." Party bureaucrats and self-promoters, fanatical and narrow-minded "priests of the cult of personality," types that will appear in Russian literature for years to come, were vividly described in this novel for the first time. The title of the novel is symbolic: The horrors of the "cult" become part of the daily routine, and the people keep silent as if nothing were happening. The novel was translated into many languages, and a recent successful Soviet film was based on it.

This year *Novy Mir* published the sequel to Bondaryov's novel *Silence*, called *The Couple*. Here the hero, Sergei Vokhminchev, is forced to quit the Mining Faculty and leave Moscow because he failed to inform his party cell that his father had been imprisoned as an "enemy of the people" on a false denunciation. In this sequel the chief characters are Sergei Vokhminchev's sister, Asya, and her husband, Kostya, who were introduced in the first part. There is a moving scene in which a half-drunk camp guard comes from Siberia to Moscow with a message from the aging Vokhminchev, and tells Asya and Kostya how they transport the prisoners: " 'Of course, the children suffer for their parents,' said Mikhail Nikiforovich, clearing his throat. 'The women also: that is, their wives. But are they to be blamed? For example, a father does something against the authorities, and the women are left to themselves in tears . . . Women, I say, suffer,' Mikhail Nikiforovich repeated . . . 'We led the column, some hundreds of them, toward the compound. And then this tumult started: From around the freight station, women came rushing from all sides, from yards and alleys and every corner, all crowding the column. They were crying, shouting and calling out names. They had come from many towns to this prison, and had been hiding somewhere. Screams, noises, laments—the women disrupted the column as they searched for their men . . . Guards began shoving, afraid somebody might escape. They clicked their safety-catches, and struck out with their rifle butts. They command the column: "On the double, march!" The column started running, and the guards smacked the women with their rifles . . . Then I heard a prisoner crying loudly, then another, then the whole column all crying: The women brought them to this—the men could not hold out. They screamed: "Why are you hitting the women? Let us say goodbye to them!" But is it permitted? The regulations do not permit it. What if somebody escapes? The guards started cursing and ordering: "Run! Run!" How is it possible not to get angry?'

" 'Shut up!' Asya's broken and hostile voice was heard. 'Stop talking, stop talking,' she repeated with disgust."

Bondaryov lives in a comfortable and spacious *dacha*. A "typical" Russian, a frank and gregarious man, he radiates decency and candor, if not a great intellect. We drank together and without realizing it consumed a whole bottle of cognac while arguing about Antonioni's pictures and whether the roots of Fascism lie in the socio-economic sphere or in a deeper, psychological realm. Bondaryov commented that Antonioni, though talented, is not yet indispensable and is premature. Humanity, Bondaryov argued, is still troubled by other problems: daily bread and a roof over one's head. My opinion was that the most important problems never trouble the "majority of humanity." Did the problem of whether the earth rotates around the sun or the sun around the earth ever trouble the "majority of humanity"? I argued that Antonioni is quite indispensable at the moment, for he shows that "daily bread and a roof over one's head" are not enough in themselves. Moreover, I said, this struggle for "bread" often shields man from the other side of the tragedy—the tragedy of his loneliness, which is much more difficult to solve than the problem of "bread and roof." Accordingly, Antonioni attacks the myth and says that "bread and roof" may have become ends in themselves, not merely the means to life.

I went on by referring to the famous critic K. Mochul'-sky who, in his book on Dostoevsky,[22] argued that the novel *Poor People* was not only a social novel: If the bitter destiny of its heroes were determined only by their poverty, Mochulsky wrote, their other problems would not be quite so insoluble. "And suppose that Makar

[22] Mochul'sky's book, one of the most important basic works on Dostoevsky, is being published in an English translation by the Princeton University Press.

Devushkin receives a big inheritance, improves his standard of living and gives material help to Varenka," I said.
"Is this the end of his sufferings? On the contrary, when
he is freed from material worries, his sufferings become
more obvious. Devushkin is unhappy not only because
he is poor: He loves Varenka, and does not have her
love in exchange."

"To pretend that 'bread' solves everything," I con-
tinued, "means running headlong into a blind alley." I
cited the fact that Sweden, which socially and economically is the most fortunate country of all, has the
highest rate of suicides. Why? Because there is no need
to struggle for an existence. On the other hand, in times
of natural disasters or war there are few suicides. That
is why Dostoevsky justified wars (in *The Diary of a
Writer*). I could not persuade Bondaryov, however. The
myth of a "Socialist paradise" has been dominant too
long in the USSR, and whoever tries to express any
doubt about it risks appearing abnormal. Even to critics
of the status quo like Bondaryov, Galileo must have
seemed bizarre when he claimed the sun was in a fixed
place and that the planet earth moved in empty space.

The same thing happened when we discussed the roots
of Fascism. The naïveté with which even intelligent
people in the USSR (except the youngest generation)
see its causes as purely economic is stupefying. As if the
Germans risked their lives in war solely to live better
economically after victory! And Bondaryov claimed just
that. I asked him if he, too, went to war for economic

reasons. He did not, of course, but the Germans . . . That was another story. We could not agree at all.

After three and a half hours our subjects and our bottle were emptied, and we parted friends. Bondaryov, like Ehrenburg and many other Soviet writers, concluded the visit with the complaint that the Yugoslav publishers did not send him copies of the Yugoslav edition of his novel *Silence*.

VLADIMIR TENDRYAKOV

Bondaryov accompanied us to Tendryakov's *dacha*. We walked around it, knocked at the door, even went inside. Nobody home. We were about to leave when suddenly, out of the bushes, a stout, blond, balding man of about forty appeared, wearing a boxer's training outfit. I thought this was the chauffeur. "Whom are you looking for?" he said.

I explained, "I am from Yugoslavia, I am Tendryakov's translator, I translated his *Three, Seven, Ace*. Well, I would like to . . ." The "chauffeur" interrupted me. "I am this Tendryakov. Please come in."

The writer, a direct man, soon was talking excitedly about the novel he was writing. Unlike other young writers of the sixties—writers like Viktor Nekrasov,

Kazakov, Nikitin, Tarasenkova, Trifonov and Dik, whose appealing topical subjects must often compensate for lack of expressive skill—Tendryakov uses strong, rich, yet concise language without apparent need for external devices. His sentences are remembered—a rare achievement for most novelists.[23]

Tendryakov does not write copiously; one feels he does nothing in a hurry. He gained fame and recognition in 1960 with *Three, Seven, Ace,* which describes a conflict among people in a backward part of Russia, a conflict that ends in murder. In this novel. Tendryakov, shows that the social order cannot solve all human problems.[24] Like all talented writers, he provokes controversy with each of his works. His very first novel. *A Tight Knot*—whose hero, Pavel Mansurov, is the kind of "useless man" not traditionally tolerated in Soviet literature (heroes must be activists)—was condemned in 1958 by the official critic Vitaly Ozerov:

"But whose destiny did we follow through 250 pages of the novel? The destiny of an able worker who evaded Leninist norms of life and wound up in a blind alley, or the destiny of a petit-bourgeois who is interesting to nobody? The novel does not give any answer to this."

---

[23] It should perhaps be noted that personal acquaintanceship (or lack of it) may color Mihajlov's literary judgment since—of the writers cited—Kazakov and Tarasenkova are generally rated as being at least equal in importance to Tendryakov.

[24] *Three, Seven, Ace* has been translated in the anthology *Dissonant Voices in Soviet Literature* (N.Y., 1962), but unfortunately the translation has been badly abridged and tampered with.

Tendryakov's short story "Miraculous" and his first play, *The White Flag*, also caused trouble. The drama was attacked by Ilichyov, the Central Committee's Secretary for ideological questions. When the work was well received abroad, however, the uproar faded. Now the play is being performed in Bratislava, and "Miraculous" even appears in school anthologies.

A similar pattern appears to be developing with his newest and, in his opinion, worthiest novel, *Foundling*. In this he describes the psychic awakening of a tough foreman of forest workers who was intentionally "forgotten" by his workers and left behind in the forest on the bank of a lake. The foreman finds a small child, and risks his own life to save it. The editor of *Novy Mir* has taken the novel to the Central Committee but he has not gotten permission to print it as yet. Tendryakov is an optimist though. "Sooner or later it will be printed," he says. According to him, things in the USSR are rapidly improving, despite the fact that a suspicion of anything new still exists. He told us laughingly that he was almost arrested in a hotel not so long ago, because a man who shared his room thought Tendryakov had poison capsules (they were crystal filters for a cigar holder) and notified the local KGB. But he should be forgiven, the writer said, because in the Soviet press there are often articles about American spies who try to poison Soviet leaders, and who usually carry their poison in capsules.

On the other hand, Tendryakov went on, there are many positive things in the USSR. He gave the reading of books as an example. Lenin, before the Revolution, observed that the average Russian read and knew more than the common people of other European nations. Tendryakov recalled how Lenin, traveling through Germany, was amazed that some of his German fellow passengers had never heard of Dürer. "Something like that would never happen in Russia," Lenin wrote. Then I told Tendryakov that during my talks with students at the Moscow Academy of Theater Art, I discovered that some had never heard of Vladimir Solovyov. The writer only shrugged his shoulders.

From this we passed to the subject of education, and again I was deeply surprised by the extent to which even the most intelligent men in the USSR had absorbed the basic premises of Stalinism. Tendryakov hotly defended the education of the "new man" in the spirit of collectivism, and his being subjected to the interests of society. "If somebody does not want to be useful to the society, we will force him to be," he said angrily. I remarked that this was only a step away from the concentration camps, and that history shows how futile it is to force people to do anything. "Fortunately," I said, "if anything educates it is personal experience, and that we are free to accept or not."

I recalled Roisman's picture *Communist*, in which a beautiful sequence illustrates my view: The hero tries to start a train bringing food to a hungry village; the train has stopped in a forest because it has run out of coal. The trainmen sit around doing nothing. When the Communist tries to interest them in chopping wood for the locomotive, they laugh. The task is indeed difficult. The

Communist starts chopping a tree, and the others only watch him. He strikes the tree with his axe all day long, stubbornly. The other men stop laughing, and then begin to get angry: "Stop this crazy work," they tell him. But when the Communist collapses from fatigue, all of them take up the axes. This, in my opinion, is the only possible education. Had the Communist tried force, he would not have succeeded. The men would have only pretended to work, feeling that they were right in their actions because it was the only way they could respond to force. This illustrates the difference between leading and ruling. Tendryakov did not agree.

The problem of education will be a painful one for Soviet society for a long time. It is difficult to overcome this contradiction: On the one hand, "man is the product of social conditions," meaning it is not man who needs to be changed, but only the conditions. On the other hand, "the new man should be educated—even by force if necessary." It is hard for men to renounce their own wrong attitudes, no matter how much has been denied them by the very principles they accept—especially if they have fought for them all their lives out of the noblest impulses. Everything new is thus characterized as the "bad inheritance of capitalistic society."

Among other things, Tendryakov told us that his friend, the Academician Kapitsa, famous as a mathematical genius, was under house arrest for eight years during the Stalin era.

Since it was already late in the evening, Tendryakov drove me and my guide back to Moscow by car.

VIKTOR SHKLOVSKY

One day, my guide and I started for the Peredelkino *dacha* settlements of writers, some 19 miles from Moscow. We went to visit Shklovsky.

Viktor Shklovsky, one of the greatest critics, theoreticians and historians of literature in our century—a poet, writer and film critic—was born in 1893 and is still active and creative. He is a cultivated writer of universal taste, an historian who moves with equal facility among the literature of the Greco-Roman, ancient Chinese, medieval or contemporary periods—certainly the greatest Russian comparative literature scholar and one of the most talented Russian essayists. Nearly all of his books have inspired stormy disputes.[25] His most important works are: *Art As a Method* (1917), *On the Theory of Prose* (1925), *The Development of the Plot* (1921), *Notes on the Prose of Russian Classics* (1959), and *Artistic Prose, Reflections, and Analyses* (1961). His book *Pro and Contra: Notes on Dostoevsky* (1957) is of special value and interest.

In debates about the theory of literature, Shklovsky opposes the sociological method (or what might better be called "sociological vulgarization") and he demonstrates that the development of art forms and styles is not directly connected with the development of society; that

[25] For a brief description of Shklovsky's theories in particular and Russian formalist criticism in general see the article by Victor Erlich in *Partisan Review* (May 1953).

it is autonomous, and that there are only certain parallels between the two. The value of an art work is, according to this view, determined by form and not by content. In 1923, Shklovsky wrote in his book *Knight's Move:* "Art was always independent of life, and never reflected the colors of the flag fluttering above the citadel." I think that he is right insofar as the "color of the flag" is identified with life. He also wrote: "I'll crush Belinsky with the legs of my writing desk." Another widely quoted statement: "The modernists are setting the world on its head not to take away one's breath, but to restore the feeling of reality." Shklovsky sees the task of art in much the same way as the great modern Russian poet, his friend Mayakovsky. He teaches us "not to believe in the present moment"; he maintains that the "future is more real than the present," and that the artist must "make the known, unknown." From this comes the theory of *ostranenie* (alienation), that is, of "shifting reality" or "making strange" in the work of art (calling to mind the theoreticians of the French "new novel"). Art is play, Shklovsky says, but there is nothing more serious and more worthy than play in life; he even makes certain analogies between chess playing and artistic creation. In the theory of literature he is considered the founder of the "science of motivation" in the criticism of art. To the question whether art must approach people and become understandable to all, or whether we have to raise ouselves to art, Shklovsky responds by pointing out the example of Leo Tolstoy—whose works "written especially for the people" are not read at all by the people and never have been; instead Tolstoy had to raise himself up to the level of *War and Peace* and to *Anna Karenina*. In his latest book, *Artistic Prose, Reflections, and Analyses* (1961) there are several excellent essays—such as those on Hemingway, on *Don Quixote*, and on *Quiet Flows the Don* by Mikhail Sholokhov—in which he finds, among other things, many elements of modernistic form: for example, the "black sun on the black sky" which Grigory Melekhov sees after Aksynya's death. In his study of the classical English novel Shklovsky points out that Sterne uses "stream of consciousness" in *Tristram Shandy*. In a long study, *On the Russian Short Story and Novel*, Shklovsky draws an interesting parallel between Tolstoy and Joyce. One of the first works of Tolstoy was the unfinished *Story of the Day Before* (1851), which would have been something like Joyce's *Ulysses* if Tolstoy had finished it, according to Shklovsky. This story, in which the conscious and subconscious states of mind of the author were described with Joycean minuteness of detail, Tolstoy left unfinished, with a note that "there are works which are easier to write than not to write." Shklovsky talks about how Tolstoy consciously tried to escape into the world of "external reality" because he understood that the "internal world," that is, "the world of oneself," is slavery and that only the renunciation of the self can bring freedom to man. In this case, the writers of the French "new novel" who also avoid description of the "internal world" could refer to Tolstoy as well.

Shklovsy was ignored and neglected for a long time,.

and it was only after 1956 that his numerous books appeared again.

Now I was going to talk to this man who was already a living legend in Russian literary thought. And as Pasternak's grave is in Peredelkino as well, I decided to visit it on the way to see Shklovsky.

Passing through the forest on the road to the "Home of Creation," the Rest Home of the Writers Union where Shklovsky lives during the summer, we came to the cemetery and went to find Pasternak's grave. A passerby sent us to a certain part of the cemetery and told us to look for three pines. We would find the poet's grave under these pines.

We wandered for a long while through the big cemetery. There were a great number of pines, but Pasternak's grave was nowhere in sight. Then some women passed by and answered our questions with another question: "Pasternak—is he that pilot?" We met two other men who not only did not know the poet's grave, but had never heard of Pasternak. Obviously, the official silence is bearing fruit. At last, an elderly woman took us to the three pines, but there was nothing to see: just some workers at the poet's grave, setting up a marble tombstone. They did not know who was paying for it.

We left the cemetery and went by narrow, asphalt paths toward the Writers' Rest Home. This is not one house, but many little wooden houses scattered among the trees; the writers who live in them take only their meals in the central building. Soon we found Shklovsky.

A short, stout man, with shaved head and mustache, he seemed much younger than his 70 years. He was sitting in bathing trunks (the sun was blazing hot) on a chair under a tree.

He received us kindly, and told us about his work. He never makes notes but writes from memory—which is really incredible considering the amount of factual material in his work. The talk turned to Dostoevsky, and Shklovsky became very animated. Hearing from Shklovsky's wife that we were talking about Dostoevsky, Mikhail Semyonovich Gus joined us (he is one of the eminent contemporary Soviet "Dostoevskiologists"). From Dostoevsky the discussion then turned to mysticism. Shklovsky told us about his friendship with Tsyolkovsky, the great Russian scientist who was a pioneer in the penetration of outer space, and who had seriously stated that he was communicating and talking with ghosts. I learned from Shklovsky that Tsyolkovsky's first mathematics teacher was Nikolai Fyodorov, one of the most enigmatic of all the Russian philosophers of the 19th century. Fyodorov noticed Tsyolkovsky's interest in mathematics and astronomy, encouraged it, and taught the boy the fundamentals of mathematical science. A strange, little-known philosopher, Nikolai Fyodorov printed all his works in only a few dozen copies because he was of the opinion that they were not fit "for everybody." He himself chose his readers. Both Tolstoy and Dostoevsky esteemed him greatly. Fyodorov's basic idea was the resurrection of all who ever lived, by scientific method. The idea was based on an original theory of relativity involving the possibility of moving in time. Shklovsky told us that Fyodorov once explained his theories about resurrection to his pupil Tsyolkovsky, and the boy asked him quite reasonably: "But how are all these people going to be squeezed on earth?" Fyodorov responded: "There are plenty of stars." This, supposedly, awakened in the boy a fascination with the possibility of flights into space, and that is how the first great theoretician of space flights was born.

During talk about the French "new novel" Shklovsky told us that he had found two unknown Tolstoy short stories which were not a bit different from Natalie Sarraute's prose.

I told them that I had found in Aleksei Remizov's *Fish Pond* (1908) several passages identical with the key scenes of Kafka's *The Trial;* Shklovsky was not aware of this.[26] He was quite interested in learning about it, and Gus, who was working on his book about modern Russian prose, immediately noted down the data I gave him. I was pleasantly surprised by the fact that a typical theoretician and historian of Socialist Realism (as Gus was, judging by his book on Dostoevsky) knew the work of Teilhard de Chardin. He said that he personally met Berdyaev when he, Gus, was a student and Berdyaev the

---

[26] Remizov's works are peopled with demons and marked by an almost baroque use of language. His favorite Russian author was the 17th-century heretic Archpriest Avvakum. He emigrated from Russia in 1921, and has yet to receive his due recognition either in Russia or abroad.

famous professor at the Academy of Free Thought in Moscow in 1919–22.

We talked about Russian philosophy, about Solovyov, Konstantin Leont'ev, Vasily Rozanov, Lev Shestov, Nikolai Lossky—about philosophers who are so little known, so unfairly neglected in their own fatherland.

I was much impressed by Shklovsky's liveliness of spirit, his varied interests and his enormous culture. When we said goodbye to Viktor Borisovich and started for Moscow, I felt that I had met one of the most cultured, most intelligent and best-educated men of our century.

BULAT OKUDZHAVA

This may be the most famous man in this vast country to-day. He is a Muscovite, a chansonnier, a balladeer, who composes and plays his own songs, accompanying himself on the guitar. His name is authentic; it is not something cooked up by the daily press—far from it, for the Soviet press is silent about him.[27] But his songs circulate in Russia, and they are sung wherever young people meet. In trains, in parks, at student parties—everywhere

[27] Mihajlov refers here to the frequent practice in the Soviet press whereby Russian writers with unusual names are presented as "our brotherly Comrades" of the various national minorities "whose blossoming culture we greet with joy and expectation!"

I heard the songs of Bulat Okudzhava. I was told that they were also popular with Murmansk sailors and in youth work camps on the endless plains of Kazakhstan.

These songs are, moreover, reaching wider and wider audiences by means of magnetic tape. Today the tape recorder plays an important role in the life of the USSR. The machines are relatively cheap, and many people have them, especially young people. The tapes thus spread from town to town all the things that the official press and radio choose not to include in their programs.

Bulat Okudzhava's situation is ambiguous. His songs are not forbidden. On the contrary, he gives frequent concerts in the cities (one was attended by 18,000 fans). But it is impossible to buy records of his songs, because none are being produced. Okudzhava told me himself that his songs have been recorded twice, but the records were never issued: At the last moment "somebody" intervened. Tapes of these songs were brought back to Poland by some Polish journalists, however, and Radio Warsaw now broadcasts Okudzhava regularly. Most harmful to the singer in his country is the fact that his songs are also broadcast by Munich's "Radio Liberty."

I did not find Okudzhava in Moscow. His mother gave me his telephone number in Leningrad and I saw him there, at the Hotel Oktyabrskaya, where I was staying. This hotel is near the Moscow Station, and since Okudzhava was leaving for Moscow that same evening, it was convenient for him to come to my room a couple of hours before his departure.

Okudzhava is a tall, thin, dark-skinned man of about

forty, who does not look like a Russian (his father was a Georgian, and his mother is Armenian). He has a mustache and sad, intelligent eyes. He reminded me somehow of descriptions of Zoshchenko, the great Russian humorist. As a young man he volunteered for service at the front, and after the War he completed studies at a teachers' institute. He taught school in a remote village for five years. His father was shot as a "Japanese spy" during the great purges; his mother was imprisoned for 19 years in one of the Siberian "female camps." (Both of them were members of the Communist Party.) She was rehabilitated in 1956, and came back to Moscow.

Okudzhava started by writing poetry, and his poems were published. Then he wrote prose, and only incidentally started singing one evening, among friends, the words of one of his own songs—improvising a melody and accompanying himself on the guitar. The song was so well received by those present that the poet immediately improvised several more melodies for his verses. Sometime later, in Moscow, his friend Lev Annensky, editor of the magazine *Znamya,* told him he had recorded Okudzhava's improvisations on a tape recorder, and that a day later several more tape copies were made because everybody at the party wanted them. And thus Okudzhava, without knowing it, entered on a career that spread his name across Russia.

Such widespread popularity draws the attention not only of lovers of beauty. Since most of Okudzhava's songs take a satirical view of life, the poet has also prompted some unpleasant warnings. But these warnings, as he himself says, are becoming less frequent. People are slowly getting used to the freer words, and Okudzhava is an optimist in this respect.

To illustrate: Several years ago his satirical song *Fools* began to circulate. The content of the ballad, briefly, is this: Everything in this world is just and honest. There is an ebb and a flow, and a sensible man for each fool. But since fools can be recognized from afar, all the people cry "Fools! Fools!" Thus, in order to spare these fools, one day all sensible men were labeled "fool." Now ever-one shouts at the sensible men: "Fools, fools!" and the real fools pass unnoticed.

Okudzhava was called before the Central Committee and was told, more or less: "You sing your songs so nicely; why did you have to go and compose this song *Fools?*" Okudzhava promised that he would not sing that song at concerts any more. A year later he composed another song, *The Black Tomcat:* A black tomcat lives in the dark gateway of our house; it's a long time since he caught any mice. Now, assisted by darkness, he preys on us instead. He does not ask for anything and he does not beg; we bring him everything ourselves and we say: "Thank you." It's probably because of this that our house is sad. We should have put an electric bulb in the gateway, but we cannot get up enough money. Again Okudzhava was called in: "You sing your songs so nicely; for example, a nice song like *Fools.* Why did you have to go and compose a song like *The Black Tomcat?*"

"Well, that's the way it goes," Okudzhava says, and his optimism is completely justified.

The situation was similar with his poems. Two years ago a publishing house accepted his collection entitled *The Midnight Trolleycar*. Somebody, however, thought the title was too pessimistic, and changed it to *The Merry Drummer*—the name of another verse in the collection. Then a dozen songs that looked suspicious to the publisher were left out. According to Okudzhava, there was nothing suspicious about these poems; they were left out, as he put it, "just in case." "Is it possible that when the poet writes the word 'glass,' he really means 'bomb'?" Okudzhava asked ironically. It was decided, at last, that the collection should not be printed at all. Then Okudzhava sent a protesting letter to Ilichyov (this reminded me of the famous Zamyatin letter to Stalin).[28] Ilichyov did not answer—but the publishing house let Okudzhava know that the collection was going to be printed for sure, and that nobody ever really thought of not printing it, and so on. In the meantime, Okudzhava wrote some more poems and added them to the collection to replace those which had been omitted. The publisher made a new choice among these poems, "just in case" again. But in the meantime, Okudzhava added more new poems—and so on, endlessly. Only recently, in the fall, Okudzhava wrote me that the collection had finally been published. I wish him luck!

Altogether Okudzhava has composed 90 songs. Yet he

---

[28] This letter, too, is printed in the 1955 New York Russian edition of Zamyatin's articles. It is unquestionably one of the most courageous documents of our times; it was published in English in the Summer 1962 issue of *Dissent*.

has not been writing them for more than a year. He has lost interest in them, and this is understandable, since he has had to repeat them so often at concerts. He is turning to prose more and more now.

A year ago *Pravda* attacked Okudzhava's novel *Lots of Luck, Kid!* (which was also translated into Serbo-Croatian).[29] However, the situation is better now, and Okudzhava is working on his new novel about (he says) the superficially funny but in fact sad adventures of a village schoolteacher.

Okudzhava, by the way, has never been abroad. When he is invited to visit Poland or Czechoslovakia, the Writers' Union always answers that Okudzhava is too busy, and that he is sorry not to be able to come. Okudzhava is fuming. He would gladly visit Yugoslavia.

Okudzhava's songs are the precious creation of Russian poetry; they will live as long as Moscow lives, because they are melodies of the city, of Moscow streets and alleys, of the trolleycars and miserable little sublet rooms, of scandalous drunken scenes in the famous Georgian restaurant *Aragvi;* and of prostitutes who gather by Pushkin's Monument in the evening. These songs are of "the living life" of Moscow; they speak of the nameless, ordinary citizens of the giant city, as in the song about a "Moscow ant," who has to pray to somebody and who therefore makes himself a god, and the one about the last

[29] *Lots of Luck, Kid!* is available in an unabridged translation in the American edition of *Pages from Tarusa.* There is an abridged translation in *Halfway to the Moon.*

trolleycar, which circles Moscow gathering up all the evening's shipwrecked.

When I have no more strength to overcome
the pain,
When despair is growing,
I jump onto the blue trolleycar,
The last one, the stray one.

And the touching of shoulders with other men in a full trolleycar helps one: "How much goodness there is in silence, in silence," goes the song.

A lot could be written about each of Okudzhava's songs, without actually defining them. They have to be heard. How can one convey, for example, the melody of the beautiful song about Arbat (a district of Moscow): "Oh, Arbat, oh Arbat, you are my religion. One could never be cured of your love, your streets could never be passed through all the way...."

These songs have explored the underworld as well. One song tells of a merry group passing through a "dive" where "pimps and prostitutes" are sitting, and how one of the pimps—a dark-haired man—"impudently looks at one of our little girls." The guest thinks, "Although I don't like to fight, I'll have to go and tell him: 'You know, pimp, our girls don't sell themselves for money.'" These are all small and "historically" unimportant tales of the tragedy and bravery of ordinary people; and of the joys, too, like the one about a girl taking a bus trip with her sweetheart (dressed in dirty work clothes) from one end of Moscow to the other. (And what is most important?

That the trip costs only twenty kopeks). There is a song about happiness appearing suddenly in the door of an attic room in the form of a beautiful woman ("Woman, Your Majesty: You must have mistaken the street, the town, the century"); another about the lives of nameless people who have unlimited credit only with "three women, three sisters, three nurses—Faith, Hope, and Charity." All this is poured out and immortalized in words and song. Long live the memory of Okudzhava, who has not forgotten that in addition to the state, history, the conflict of the social systems, and gigantic buildings, man also matters!

The song *Roosters* is interesting: Every day at dawn the roosters crow—but there are no more fools responding to them. All the heroes of Okudzhava's songs could agree with the words of Schweik in Brecht's play *Schweik in the Second World War,* who responds to a speech about the "great historical epoch" in which we are living: "I piss on this great epoch."

The song *About the Paper Soldier* tells of a soldier who wanted to change the world so that "everybody would be happy," but forgot that he was made of paper:

We didn't believe him,
And we kept silent about our secrets,
Why? Because—
He was made of paper.

The soldier was constantly giving the cry, "Into battle, into the fire"; finally he took a step into the flames and burned because he was made of paper.

Undoubtedly, Okudzhava's songs alarm all those who love the marching step and military music. "A lot of fools are still going to enjoy lively soldier songs," Okudzhava sings. He has written many songs about war and the Army. But his attitude toward war must repel over-patriotic spirits; he ridicules every war and every army. One of his songs relates the tale of a king who went to war. The queen gave him a little sack full of biscuits and some salt in a piece of paper. The king divided his army, ten soldiers and a sergeant, into two parts: He left the cheerful soldiers behind the front as attendants, and sent the gloomy ones into battle. The gloomy soldiers were shot, and the cheerful ones came back victoriously with their booty—a sack of honey-cakes. The end of the song is this: "There is no sense in being sad, because for the sad one there is no sense in living, and there would not be enough honey-cakes for everyone, anyway."

One of the most famous Okudzhava songs is *The Song about a Soldier:*

I'll take the cloak, the bag and helmet
Painted with camouflage,
I'll march along the bumpy streets;
How easy it is to become a soldier,
*   to become a soldier.*

I'll forget all the domestic worries
I need neither work nor pay
I go and play with an automatic rifle
How easy it is to be a soldier,
*   to be a soldier.*

And if something is wrong, it's not our
   worry;
As the saying goes: "The fatherland commands!"
How nice it is to be blamed for nothing,
To be an ordinary soldier, an ordinary soldier.

It is worth noting that at his concerts Okudzhava announces the song as *The Song about an American Soldier*.

The Song about Lyonka Korolyov is a very popular one. It tells of the youth Lyonka, who was highly respected by his comrades and was called "the King" because he always offered his "imperial hand" to anyone in trouble, and helped his fellow man. When the war started, "the King" put his cap on his head as a real king puts on his crown, and went off to the war. He did not come back, the song concludes, but it is impossible to believe that he was killed, it is impossible to imagine Moscow without a man like Lyonka, "the King."

Concerning responsibility for the war, Okudzhava sings:

The first war—it's nobody's fault,
The second war—it's somebody's fault,
The third war—it's my fault.

Russia was always known for the richness of its masterful songs (let us note only Vertinsky), and Okudzhava's case proves this holds true today as well. Immense harm is being done to Russian culture by those who stop the production of his records, who censor radio broadcasts or hamper the publication of Okudzhava's songs. But as long as there are such talents as Bulat Okudzhava persisting in their work, Russian art and Russian music will live —in spite of everything.

THE APOLOGIST OF ABSTRACTIONISM

Vladimir Nikolaevich Turbin is one of the most popular lecturers at Moscow University. Wherever there was talk about art and literature, about formalism and modernism, I always heard the name Turbin. I had never heard of him before, and my friends from MGU had great difficulty in providing me with Turbin's book—in the end, they let me borrow a copy, but only for two days. I am not sorry for the time I spent reading it. "The Turbin case" shows once more how little we know of what is happening in the USSR.

In 1961 Turbin published *Comrade Time, Comrade Art,* which dealt with the problem of modernism in literature. In this poetically written book, Turbin effectively defended modernism, including Cubism, relying chiefly upon the early Mayakovsky and the Russian Futurists for his examples. Basically, his thesis could be summed up as follows: When one is hungry, material affluence is a blessing, but when one becomes sated, other aspects of life become paramount; and this principle also applies to art. Progress in art consists not of endless augmentation of received conventions but of the transformation of what is essential to art. Thus the progress of art does not lie in the augmentation of so-called Realism, but in essential change—modernism. The motto of the book is, appropriately, a few verses by Mayakovsky:

Out of the distance of time
Appears something different,
The third revolution—
The revolution of spirit!

The book was printed in an edition of 22,000, an absurdly small number for the USSR, and it is impossible to find a copy today. After the book was published there was, of course, a lot of excitement: Ilichyov, writing in *Pravda,* called Turbin "the apologist of abstractionism."

During my meeting with Turbin, a robust, youngish man with grey hair, I asked him what the situation is now. Turbin is another optimist. In spite of Ilichyov's attack, he was not forced to leave the University. "Times are different now," he said. He is now preparing a new book, a book of identical inspiration though, he says, an even more radical one. There is also a possibility that the first book will be reprinted.

The most important developments in the spiritual life of Russia are being suppressed or ignored, and so Turbin's book, which in many ways anticipates and surpasses R. Garaudy's *Realism without Shores,* remains completely unknown to the world. Once again, a talented Slav foregoes his place in the cultural life of humanity. It is nothing new for Russia, of course. If we remember how

Shestov, Berdyaev, Remizov, Zamyatin, Rozanov, Fyodorov, Leont'ev, Solovyov and many other artists and
philosophers, both of this century and of the last, were
ignored in their own country, we can see that a two-
century-old tradition still lives.

Still, to use Zamyatin's words: "The heretics are the
salt of the earth; the life of the universe is sustained by
them," and however much they are hushed or silenced,
"they will always be heard from again." Or, as Turbin
says: "The pupil who is disobedient and bold, who dares
to argue with his teacher, is the more necessary to
art. . . ."

EVGENY VINOKUROV

Not far from the Yugoslav Embassy in Vorosky Street is
the Writers' Home, seat of the Union of Soviet Writers,
along with various international commissions and depart-
ments. The big hall in the central building is used for
festivals, conferences and commemorations, and in the
basement club room they serve espresso coffee. It is the
only place in all Moscow where the coffee is prepared
properly. As Ehrenburg told me: "Coffee is cooked in
Russia like borscht."

I passed the body of Samuil Marshak—lying in state
in the hall, like Lenin's—and went down to the club

to have coffee. All the walls of the club are covered with drawings and caricatures, and with verses by contemporary poets, just like the painters' club on Kalemegdan in Belgrade.

In the Writers' Home I had a meeting with Evgeny Vinokurov, a poet somewhat older than (and not as noisy as) the "galaxy of the young," but a talented and original Russian lyricist. Today Vinokurov is probably the only philosophically inclined poet of the Russian Parnassus, and his poetry in free, rhymeless verses is nearest to Western European poetry.

A few days before my arrival in Moscow, Vinokurov's latest book of poetry, *Music*, had just been published. This somewhat un-Russian volume seems strange in the oceans of published and collected verse. There is not a single poem in it on social, patriotic or revolutionary subjects! Moreover, it has the deftness of a master, and to this we may ascribe the fact that Vinokurov, of all contemporary Russian poets, is the one most frequently translated. This year translations of his poetry were published in Italy, Bulgaria, Czechoslovakia and Hungary. In Russian poetry Vinokurov could be compared only with Tiutchev, whom, beside Pasternak, Tsvetaeva, Mandelstam and Zabolotsky, he considers his teacher. In the West he can be compared only with Rimbaud.

Vinokurov refuses to go to the poetry meetings frequented by his colleagues—Evtushenko, Rozhdestvensky, Akhmadulina and others. "One should read poetry only when alone," the poet told me. He is a small, fat man, about forty, whose appearance belies his vocation.

"Anything that is liked by everybody is always bad," he added. His poem *Rhythm* is characteristic:

Drivers are scared of suicides.

Once, seeing a barber
Sharpening his razor on a strap,
I thought how rhythm rules the world.

Rhythm was assigned to the world,
The world is wound up as far as it will go
As is done with watches.

The night inevitably
Replaces the day.
Signals are blinking in the streets.
A teaspoon is systematically turned around
In the glass of the watchman
Of the Museum of Oriental Cultures.
The moon directs

The ebb and flow of the ocean.
Buttons on a vest are rhythmical.
Mother, uncovering her heavy breasts,
Rocks the child.
All that is alive is pulsating, like stars.

But who knows
What idea
May strike man's mind?

As a motto for his latest collection, the poet took Zabolotsky's line: "Word—become music." In contemporary Russian poetry Vinokurov is the only one who composes crystal, "acoustical" verses, as if he were a French Symbolist instead of a contemporary Russian poet.

I don't believe that Evgeny Vinokurov is ever going to become a popular poet in his country. And that's why he is not going to be strongly attacked. Russians are used to the other kind of poetry, so-called *engagé* poetry (in whatever direction). And Vinokurov is a solitary philosopher for whom the world is a complete and constant puzzle about which people know so little they do not dream that it is a wonder:

> *I wish to write a book one day,*
> *In which there would be everything about time,*
> *About its nonexistence.*
> *That past and future are*
> *One and the same—everything is present.*
> *I think that all people—*
> *The ones who live and the ones who have lived,*
> *And the ones who have not yet lived*
> *Are all living in this moment!*

ILYA EHRENBURG

For the first time in Moscow, I looked at walls completely covered with original paintings by modern artists: Picasso, Chagall, Braque. No, they were not in a gallery, they were in the apartment of Ilya Ehrenburg.

Ehrenburg is, really, a young old man. The body ceases to obey the spirit and the writer walks slowly, but the eyes gleam vividly and the tongue is fiery; witty sarcasm and ironic comments—all this makes a striking impression.

The day before my visit, Ehrenburg flew in from Zurich, where he had stopped on the way from Italy, and immediately after my visit he was going to his *dacha* in the settlement Ierusalim (where Chekhov once lived), some 37 miles from Moscow. Thus I was lucky to find Ehrenburg in Moscow, for it was impossible for me to travel to his *dacha*. (I had spent all my rubles, and could not borrow even a kopek from our Embassy. Apparently money was always loaned to Yugoslavs in Moscow until several years ago when a theater director from Zagreb did not return a borrowed sum, and the Embassy decided not to lend money to anybody anymore.)

Smoking excellent Cuban cigars and drinking real Turkish coffee, surrounded by masterpieces of modern painting, Ehrenburg performed (he is used to his successes with audiences) a series of exhibitions and acrobatics with his sharp and elastic wit.

It started with Yugoslavia. "Oh, it is obvious that you are a Socialist country," he said, smiling. "I have heard that you published my *Jurenito,* but nobody sent me a copy of the book. That never happens in Europe." Last year, after a delay of three and a half decades, *Julio Jurenito* was finally published in the USSR in the first volume of Ehrenburg's *Collected Works*—cut, of course; the publishers omitted the chapter about Jurenito's visit to Lenin in the Kremlin.

"You see," Ehrenburg said, "all our publishers are suffering from hypocrisy. They believe that if they omit every allusion to physical love from books, people will really think that children are found in cabbages instead of being born of women. Not so long ago, judging by our films and books, a young man and a young woman could think of nothing better to do than to sing patriotic songs and hold hands." I asked him how he explained recent Soviet puritanism—in the twenties, there was unprecedented freedom in human relations in Russia, while to get a divorce in the USSR now is almost as difficult as in Italy. Any risqué or daring scenes in foreign films are cut as if under the scrutiny of a Vatican censor. Ehrenburg thinks this is the consequence of a great number of people moving from villages into towns at the beginning of the thirties, and of the general social-political reaction at the time of "the cult of the personality."

The talk passed from one thing to another, and I found that Ehrenburg knows of the contemporary Yugoslav painters (he mentioned Lubarda, Tartalja) but that he had a very poor opinion of Yugoslav abstraction—he thinks that Polish abstraction is incomparably better. As regards contemporary Soviet visual arts, Ehrenburg says that because of their "isolation," it more and more often happens that young Soviet painters discover abstraction all by themselves, and that this is sad, for if they were not handicapped by this isolation they could adapt quickly to the fifty-year-old tradition of modern art, and progress from there. "In this way," he said, "we now have a lot of grade-school students in modernism, when we could have had masters."

"Now I am not afraid of anything any more, I am too old," he said, and surprised me with his frank ridicule of Khrushchev: "He saw a female nude for the first time at the exhibition of young Moscow modernists in the autumn of 1962." (It is well known that at this exhibition the Party delegation headed by the Premier announced an open war on modern artists.)

After that, my host described vividly his encounters with Lev Shestov and Andrei Bely in Berlin in 1922. He talked to Stalin only once, by telephone, and saw him once from a short distance.[30] Ehrenburg thinks that, in the end, Stalin was a more important personality than Hitler. He told me many more things: that he likes Chekhov best, that the contemporary young writers are maturing too late. And everything would have ended nicely if our talk had not passed to a theme on which my opinion was completely contradictory to Ehrenburg's. Bit by bit, we got into such a tussle that instead of the pre-arranged one hour, I stayed for over three hours.

I was provoked, because it seemed to me that in dis-

---

[30] Ehrenburg is quite touchy about his "special position" under Stalin—at a time when many Soviet writers and most Jewish Soviet writers were being shipped to concentration camps—and in his conversations with foreigners he frequently stresses the fact that he did not really know Stalin.

cussing the most essential problem of humanity, the brilliant Ehrenburg's spirit rudely betrayed him, and that I was suddenly faced by a man of predictable Soviet mentality, blind to all arguments and empirical facts. This was the problem: Talking of this and that, Ehrenburg joked about the domestic capabilities of Russian women, busy reorganizing the world (he said), and incompetent at boiling good coffee. Thinking that I had seen women everywhere in the USSR working on the most rugged kind of man's work (construction, ditch-digging, on the railways, driving taxis, etc.), I asked Ehrenburg what he thought of the aphorism of the famous Polish satirist Stanislaw Lec: "Socialism is hell for women"? And further, had the women's *right* to equal work with men in the USSR transformed itself into an *obligation* to work outside of the family, which, in fact, means twice as much work for the majority of women? Ehrenburg avoided a direct answer, and started telling me that in the future (Oh, this beautiful future!) the machines are going to liberate man from work, that people are going to have more free time which will have to be spent somehow, and that two things are going to play great roles in the emotional and psychic culture of liberated humanity: art and women.

This I could not swallow.

I think that there is nothing uglier than this vision of a socially reformed humanity which has no other goals but maintaining this same "high life," which consists of the education of the emotions. "Oh, then," said Ehrenburg, "people will read a lot, listen to music, conduct intelligent conversations, discover the 'secrets of nature.' And the main thing is—there would be no more wars." I recalled a thought of the great 19th century Russian philosopher, Konstantin Leont'ev, who, horrified by a vision of the "orderly ant-hill," wrote: "Isn't it horrible and offensive to think that Moses went up to Sinai, that the Greeks built their graceful Acropolis, that the Romans fought their Punic Wars, that the handsome genius Alexander, in his feathered helmet, crossed the Granicus and fought at Arbela, that the Apostles preached, martyrs suffered, poets sang, painters painted, and knights fought at tournaments only so that the French, or German, or Russian *petit-bourgeois*, in his ugly, comical clothes, could live without care, 'individually,' or 'collectively,' on the ruins of all that past greatness? . . . It would be a shame for humanity if this sinister ideal of the universal rewards of trifling work and petty prose should triumph forever."

Oh, then people will read books, play on harps, and look at or create pictures (or as Mayakovsky wrote: "They will plough the land, they will compose verses"). It is wonderful, perhaps, and educational; but I wouldn't want to be living then. The struggle for Socialism is nice, but Socialism without struggle—that is a cemetery. I said all this to Ehrenburg, and he replied that science will solve everything one day, even the problem of boredom. I claimed that there is nothing more horrible than science for, giving power over nature to man (knowledge being power), it takes away the possibility of *love;* it separates man from nature and erects a fence around him. This is, in fact, the "Eastern sin": In this opposition between nature and man, man becomes mortal, and time is born. When there is no wall of power and war between him and life, there is no more death, no more time. There is eternity. And all our science is enclosing man more and more in the solitude of knowledge. The bringing about of the orderly ant-hill where there would be no more struggle (it is only struggle that breaks the chains of consciousness and puts man in touch with life, with essence, or, in religious terminology, with God) would be the final death of life, of mankind. That is why open mysticism is incomparably more vital, for it recognizes the right of nature and of life to remain secret, and to be discovered only when they wish it.

I cited Tolstoy who wrote in 1884: "I am convinced that the history of so-called scientific work in our famous centuries of European civilization will, in a couple of hundred years, represent an inexhaustible source of laughter and sorrow for future generations. The learned men of the small Western part of our European continent lived for several centuries under the illusion that the eternal blessed life was the West's future. They were interested in the problem of when and where this blessed life would come. But they never thought of how they were going to make *their* life better."

And all this ended with Ehrenburg saying that he thought the same way in his youth, but that he had become wiser. Finally, he said that I was a kind of fanatic—

"the same as our dogmatists, only on another ideological basis."

Thus our dispute was unresolved. On my departure, Ehrenburg was rather cool and looked at me angrily. It is strange that Ehrenburg, who in 1921 in his great *Julio Jurenito* was conscious of all the pretense and masks of historical process, has come to believe seriously today in the myth of the orderly ant-hill where all troubles will have been eliminated by science.

LAKSHIN AND SOLZHENITSYN

I visited one of the editors of the most representative Soviet literary magazine, *Novy Mir*, V. I. Lakshin, in his office. As with Dudintsev before, I got into trouble with Lakshin too. We made an appointment for 5 P.M., but I arrived from my visit with Ehrenburg only at 7 P.M.— Ehrenburg had asked me to come and see him at 4 P.M., telling me that he had only one hour for conversation since he was preparing to leave for his *dacha* that same day. However, owing to the quarrel, I stayed until seven, telephoning Lakshin twice from Ehrenburg's apartment, making excuses and promising to come and see him within the next five minutes. The offices of *Novy Mir* are only a hundred yards or so from Ehrenburg's house. I arrived at his office terribly late—even in a metropolis like Moscow, this represents a terrible offense. It was all the more embarrassing since Lakshin, like many other Muscovites, lives in his *dacha* in the summer, commuting every day by electric train.

For these reasons, I had a chance to see two Lakshins: one angry, dry and cold, and the other (some time later) open, passionate and likable. Lakshin is a young man, about thirty-five, with a non-Russian aquiline nose and an extremely penetrating look behind his glasses. He is a typical throwback to the time of the First International. He won great popularity this year because of his important essay, "Ivan Denisovich, His Friends and His Enemies," published in *Novy Mir* (No. 1, 1964), in which he brilliantly defended Solzhenitsyn from increasingly frequent attacks.[31] After this essay, Lakshin was attacked in almost all of the Soviet press. Fortunately, however, there was only noise, and no unpleasant consequences for the critic. "Nowadays, there is nothing administrative that could be done to anyone here at *Novy Mir*," he told me, "since an attack against one of us would automatically mean an attack on all the editors of the magazine." That would, of course, also mean an attack against Tvardovsky, the editor-in-chief. It is well known that today Tvardovsky, is one of the few eminent non-joiners of the Writers' Union, so that he is in a position to play an extremely

[31] Excerpts from this article have been translated in the sourcebook *Khrushchev and the Arts*—1962–64 (MIT, 1965).

positive role in the liberalization of intellectual life in the Soviet Union.

After Lakshin's essay on Solzhenitsyn's novel was published and after all the turmoil it stirred up, the young critic received 150 letters a day in which readers praised his courage and expressed their support for him. When I asked why he doesn't publish these letters, he told me that the editors do not want to localize the debate around Solzhenitsyn. "Whenever they attack us," he said, "we publish something even sharper instead of going on the defensive, so that the debate is constantly transferred from one object to another."

Characteristically, he told me that in the USSR there is a widely repeated saying nowadays: "Tell me your attitude about Ivan Denisovich, and I will tell you who you are."

According to Lakshin, Solzhenitsyn is writing a long novel at his home in Ryazan.[32] To the editor of *Novy Mir*, Solzhenitsyn is the most important figure in Russian literature since the war. I told him about my essay, "The House of the Dead in Dostoevsky and Solzhenitsyn" that was about to be published in our magazine *Forum*. He was very interested, and later I sent copies of the magazine to him and to Lev Annensky, editor of *Znamya*. They never received them. Evidently the censors remain suspicious.

[32] There have been (as yet unconfirmed) reports that Solzhenitsyn has written a play which the *Sovremennik* Theater was unable to get permission to produce. Some prose poems by Solzhenitsyn were smuggled to the West and appeared in English in *The New Leader*, January 18, 1965.

Part III

VOZNESENSKY

At our first meeting Andrei Voznesensky astonished me. Apparently he had heard about me a year ago. In the spring of 1963, I had published an article on contemporary Russian poetry in *Vjesnik*[33] in which I had called him the most promising young poet in the Soviet Union, and had named the much older Leonid Martynov as the greatest contemporary Russian poet. A friend of Voznesensky's, a journalist in the German Democratic Republic, had translated my article for him over the phone. It really is a small world.

The club in the House of Writers was closed that night for some unknown reason, so we went to the Actors' Club. It is a modern and exclusive night club, the only one in Moscow open till 2 A.M., but it is not accessible to all. However, Voznesensky is well known in Moscow and the doorkeeper let us in.

Voznesensky is an architect by profession, but concerns himself only with literature. Of course, he is forced to waste much time translating languages of numerous national groups in the Soviet Union, and his translations are often better than the originals. The poet has a very young, almost child-like appearance, despite the fact that he is 30 years old. He adopts poses, but with such sincere naïveté that it does not matter. He gave me a collection of his poems on which he wrote: "A. Voznesensky, Moscow, 20th century." To my question—"Are you a member

[33] A daily newspaper published in Zagreb.

129

of the Party?"—he answered that I obviously did not
know the history of contemporary Russian literature very
well, since I was not familiar with his statement: "Like
Mayakovsky, I am not a member of the Communist
Party. . . ."[34]

Altogether Voznesensky left the most pleasant impression on me. In spite of his general immaturity (Ehrenburg remarked about him to me: "Andryusha is still a
boy; these days poets begin their careers at the age at
which Pushkin, Lermontov, Esenin and Mayakovsky ended
theirs"), he surprised me with his wide intellectual
horizon and his excellent knowledge of contemporary
Western European literature.

We talked about Kafka, Joyce, T. S. Eliot, Simone Weil,
Teilhard de Chardin, and about many things which are
terra incognita for the other Soviet writers. Voznesensky
was the one who informed me that *The Trial* was already
in print, and that the translation is excellent. He also told
me that T. S. Eliot will not be translated for a long time;
that Pasternak's collected works are in the process of
preparation for the press; that young people are accepted
into the Writers' Union, thanks to the intercession of an
average poet but remarkable man—Stephan Shchipachyov; that Evtushenko and Rozhdestvensky went on a
cruise of the North Sea for a month; and much else.

Naturally, Voznesensky's "spiritual father" is Pasternak, whom the young poet knew personally for a long

[34] This statement was supposedly made by Voznesensky at a rather
stormy Writers' Union meeting held in the Kremlin on March 7, 1963.
cf., *Literaturnaya Gazeta* (March 30, 1963).

time. As a high school student he used to visit him often, he said. Pasternak would read him parts of *Doctor Zhivago*, then still in manuscript form. (I recalled another of Ehrenburg's sarcastic remarks: "Andryusha is developing in the shadow of Pasternak. No doubt, it is a nice shadow, but still a shadow. Incidentally, when the clamor against Pasternak was raised Andryusha was bravely silent and did not take a stand in the defense of his teacher.")

Until late at night we sat in the Actors' Club. Our conversation was interrupted only by numerous greetings directed to Voznesensky; judging from this, all Moscow's "golden youth" knows him. In general, while the popularity of Evtushenko is slowly declining, Voznesensky is being read more and more, and I don't doubt that in the near future he will become the most popular poet of the young intellectual generation.

Voznesensky is more intellectual than emotional, with a technical manner of poetic expression (not thinking!) that is stylistically close to the early Mayakovsky and Pasternak. Ideologically, he is an anti-Socialist Realist; he is a poet excited more by synthetic fabrics than the hoary Russian birch tree. This disposition can be seen in his book of poems *40 Lyric Digressions from the Poem "The Triangular Pear,"* and his approach is exactly what most attracts the young educated generation these days.

The very existence of a Voznesensky today bears out the prophecy of the philosopher Nikolai Berdyaev, who in the twenties wrote of the time when science and technology would dominate the minds of the masses, and the most talented men of the intelligentsia would turn in the other direction—toward a new mysticism. Voznesensky triumphantly told me about the well-known Soviet mathematician and designer of electronic computers, Andrei Kolmogorov, who for several years analyzed texts and sent his assistant to poetry-readings with the intention of finding the "linguistic key" to versification and constructing a computer which would "replace" various poets. Naturally, he failed; the effort was successful only with the poet Vladimir Khotov, an author of stereotyped Socialist-Realist jingles.

Voznesensky agreed with me that Leonid Martynov is indeed one of the most significant living Russian poets. At one point in his life he spent several years in one of the northern concentration camps, and he would introduce himself with the words: "Leonid Martynov, Enemy of the People." Martynov was born in 1905. He began to write poetry relatively late, at the age of thirty-five. But of course his work was suppressed and he became known publicly only in 1956, together with the generation of young poets—Evtushenko, Akhmadulina, Voznesensky, Zhirmunskaya, etc. In my opinion his symbolic poem, "The River Silence," is the best Russian poem of the period from 1929 to 1956.[35] Concerning the younger poets,

[35] Martynov's *Reka Tishina* is an outstanding poem by an important poet. Its symbolism may be taken both personally and historically; it concludes: "There is no river silence/ The silence has been broken./ It is your fault./ No!/ It is your happiness./ You broke it yourself,/ That deepest of silences,/ In which you were held captive." With all due respect for Martynov's poem, however, it is difficult to accept the judgment which Mihajlov makes of it when one considers the poetry written by Akhmatova, Pasternak, Zabolotsky—to name but three—in the period he cites. *Reka Tishina* was written in 1929.

Voznesensky stressed the importance of Novella Matveeva, as had Dudintsev and Vinokurov. We also agreed
in our attitudes toward Russian classicism. Voznesensky
likes Dostoevsky and does not like Gorky.

The poet wanted to read me a passage from his latest
poem, "Oza,"[36] which he regards highly. ("Believe me,
Misha, I would give my life for this poem without hesitation.") But because it was already very late, he sketched
for me only its outline. The poem is the lyric diary of a
physicist, a confession of his love (found in a hotel); one
of its basic themes is a battle against an "evil" and for a
"good" technology. Later, back in Yugoslavia, while listening one evening to the Soviet radio program "Youth,"
I happened to hear Voznesensky reading passages from
this poem. His voice sounded impressive when he repeated about 10 times the words "Ave Oza," with which a
number of lines begin. "Oza" is an anagram of the name
Zoya. I think that the poem has great poetic power, and
the influence of surrealism can be sensed in it (Mayakovsky's suicide bullet returns from the poet's chest into
his gun). Voznesensky intended to print the poem in the
magazine *Znamya,* although he was not sure that it would
be accepted. However, the trend of events in the Soviet
Union today does not lead one to think that the poem will
be suppressed.

[36] Voznesensky's "Oza," which has since been published in the Soviet
Union, appeared in an English translation in the Spring, 1965 number
of the *Northwestern Tri-Quarterly,* in a special issue devoted to
creativity in the Soviet Union.

ZAGORSK

Forty-five miles from Moscow lies the little town of Zagorsk, home of the Troitse-Sergeeva Monastery, a 14th century complex of churches and monasteries.[37] Although foreigners may not go farther than thirty kilometers [approximately nineteen miles] from Moscow without permission, my official guide allowed me to go to Zagorsk alone because he was busy that afternoon.

It is a little town of picturesque, lush greenery. One can find no place to sit down to write a postcard or to rest, however, because in accordance with the town's custom, there are no restaurants or cafeterias of any kind —people here do not "waste time." On a little hill encircled with an ancient wall stands the elevated *lavra* with about ten church cupolas. The State Museum of Atheism is located in several of the buildings at the very center of the complex. People come from distances of hundreds of kilometers to see the *lavra*, and the churches in it are always overcrowded. Many foreigners also go there on pilgrimage. The Museum of Atheism, by its position amid the cluster of churches, symbolizes the relationship of the state and religion.

Of course, the jarring presence of the museum in no way encourages unenlightened believers to become atheists. On the contrary, the museum irritates; it provokes not merely revulsion but the desire to cross oneself publicly in front of it, even if for the first time in one's

[37] The Troitse-Sergeeva Monastery was founded about 1335.

life. Within the monastery it is an arrogant symbol of authority; it represents something respectable only for the "cult people," who pass by it many times a day. This attitude of the State toward religion, that is, denying people the right to determine of their own free will what is true and what is false, simply fortifies and stimulates religious sects.

The Soviet newspapers are full of anti-religious articles, pamphlets, and proclamations. This year the Central Committee has already held two plenary sessions dedicated to the struggle against religion. Baptists are gaining ground every day, energized by intimidation, and new nests of the sect are being discovered, especially among workers. It is hard to understand who are the more fanatical in the Soviet Union, members of the religious sects, or atheists who are fighting them. For, as André Gide has remarked (and Berdyaev, too), there never was any atheism in the Soviet Union: Atheism is a complete indifference toward religious phenomena; the questioning of God simply does not enter the sphere of the atheistic spirit. But the continuous, fanatical anti-religious battle in the Soviet Union demonstrates something else —that with the Soviets it is not at all a question of atheism, but of *anti-theism*. And it is a bloody battle. A few years ago, indeed, a Jesuitical method of combat was introduced, the so-called "individual enlightening" of persons who are discovered to be religious. To such a person a mentor (or two) is assigned whose duty it is to enlighten his protegé constantly—at work, in the club, even at home. Thus the psychological torture is intensified.

In this respect Party ideologist Leonid Ilichyov surpassed Stalin. During World War II, Stalin was forced to allow a certain amount of religious freedom. With money received for precious religious objects sold in the United States, tanks were bought for two divisions, and until 1944, when Stalin was finally sure of victory and thought it no longer necessary to cater to the religious feelings of members of the Red Army, there were tank battalions with white crosses signifying the two Soviet divisions "Saint Aleksandr Nevsky" and "Saint Dimitry Donskoy." After the War, anti-religious pressure became more severe than it had been between the two wars. As is well known, the last years of Stalin's life were the hardest years in the history of the Soviet Union. Yet not even Stalin thought of introducing "individual enlightenment" for religious believers. This was an invention of recent years.

In the spring of 1964, the Plenum of the Central Committee accepted Ilichyov's proposal to introduce atheism as a compulsory subject in the curriculum of all high schools and universities. It was at that point that the previously devoted leading French Marxist R. Garaudy, in the name of the French Communist party, abandoned Moscow and took a stand against Ilichyov. The "negative Catholicism" of the "Holy Mother Moscow Marxist Church" is self-evident; but that it is a travesty on religion, and that it is really an attempt (fortunately unsuccessful) to destroy the last remains of free will in man is proved by the methods of the struggle against religion.

The Soviet kiosks are crowded with the most vulgar

"atheistic" literature: *Amusing Gospel, Entertaining Bible*. The magazine *Science and Religion* carries stupid mockeries on the possibility of free religious consciousness in man, in articles titled "Is There a God?," "This Liar—Jesus Christ," "Behind the Walls of the Spiritual Academy," etc. Not only is this terribly stupid, it is full of poisonous hate. Understandably, the effect of it is the opposite of that which is desired. This past year *Komsomolskaya Pravda* described how nine high school girls from one of Moscow's high schools "fled" to a monastery. Poor girls, they probably had some fanatic "godfighter" atheist for an instructor or for a home-room teacher. When one sees all these stupidities, one feels like running away to a monastery for spite. Never was and never will anything be created in a man by force. Fortunately, as Berdyaev says: "Truth makes man free, but man must freely accept the Truth; he cannot be forced to accept it. Forced goodness is no longer good; it turns into evil."

RUSSIAN PHILOSOPHY

Listening to the magnificent choirs in the monastery I remembered that it was in this place that Konstantin Leont'ev, one of the most significant, daring and original Russian minds of all times, spent the last days of his life. (It is less known that Leont'ev was also a talented story teller. His novel *The Egyptian Dove*, once widely read, deserves a place in any anthology of world literature.)[38] Also, I was reminded of my conversation with Viktor Shklovsky in which we spoke of Russian philosophy being almost unknown. I surprised him with the statement that in Zagreb, philosophy students study Nikolai Lossky; in his own homeland no one knows anything about this philosopher. I talked to a large number of Soviet students, as I mentioned before, who had never heard the name Vladimir Solovyov! Everybody knows about Berdyaev and Dmitri Merezhkovsky only because the polemics against them still go on. Yugoslavia could play an important cultural role if, say, a collection of Russian philosophy were added as a 13th volume to our excellent *Collected Philosophy*.

Almost all Russian philosophers are still on the index (the "black sheet")—from Konstantin Leont'ev, Nikolai Fyodorov, Vladimir Solvyov, Apollon Grigorev (a "Bergsonian," several decades before Bergson), Nikolai Danilevsky (with his famous work *Russia and Europe*, a predecessor of Oswald Spengler) to Vasily Rozanov, Nikolai Lossky, Ivan Il'in, Vladimir Ern, Simon Frank, Georges Florovsky, Vasily Zenkovsky, Gustav Shpet, Sergei Bulgakov, Pyotr Struve, Nikolai Berdyaev, and Lev Shestov. And since, besides Nikolai Chernyshevsky, Plekhanov,

---

[38] Leont'ev's novels have never been translated into English, but there is a good short survey-article on Leont'ev's fiction by George Ivask (*Slavic Review*, December 1961). Ivask characterizes Leont'ev's novels as being basically narcissistic and exemplifying an admixture of "black Christianity" and "bright paganism."

Lenin, and Anatoly Lunacharsky, Russia had no other great Marxist philosophers (they are the only ones recognized), one gets the impression that the greatest Slavic nation has no philosophy.[39]

Yet original Russian philosophy, which is full of mysticism and anti-materialism, and in many respects is apolitical—in the persons of Shestov, Berdyaev and Rozanov—today influences much contemporary Western European philosophical thought. And we, children of one of the Slavic countries, hear about the existence of Russian philosophy—from the West.[40] (I recall how badly I felt when I discovered that in the library in Novi Sad, the numerous works of Nikolai Berdyaev, published in Paris, still had uncut pages.)

It is most interesting that the rehabilitation of Russian philosophy is prevented not by lack of interest at the bottom, but by pressure from the top because of the present political situation. Vladimir Solovyov, Danilevsky and many other Russian philosophers, for example, long ago foresaw the conflict between Russia and China in the 20th century. Solovyov, in his famous book *Three Conversations About War, Progress and the End of the World's History,* and also in his famous *Story About*

---

[39] Many of the writers cited here would be considered more properly theologians, cultural historians, critics, etc., than "philosophers" in the usual sense of that term.

[40] Twelve volumes of Berdyaev's philosophical and critical works are available in American paperback translations. The best-known are *Destiny of Man, Dostoevsky, Dream and Reality,* and *The Meaning of the Creative.*

Antichrist, cites in great detail the causes of unavoidable conflict in the future between the two great nations.[41]

It is possible that at a given moment the Soviet government will remember Solovyov, Berdyaev, and other authentic Russian thinkers in order to mobilize national feelings, just as in World War II Stalin openly invoked St. Dimitry Donskoy and St. Aleksandr Nevsky although in the first years after the Revolution they had been anathematized as symbols of the Russian Orthodox autocracy. (Apropos of this, I compared some Russian magazines from the second half of the 19th century with some contemporary Russian magazines. I was perplexed by the decline in spiritual and intellectual powers during the last hundred years. However, the sharpness of this decline can be a good thing: Every renaissance begins that way!)

ANTI-SEMITISM

In the Soviet Union, unquestionably, anti-Semitic forces do exert strong pressure. Anti-Semitism has always been strong in Russia, and though efforts are being made to subdue it, this has in no way cured the disease. When in early 1964 the European press announced with fanfare the appearance of Trofim Kichko's "Judaism Without

[41] This work has been translated in *A Solovyov Anthology* (London, 1950).

Embellishment," a typical anti-Semitic book,[42] many people in the Soviet Union were surprised. It is a known fact that a large number of Jews took part in the October Revolution. The most prominent were Leon Trotsky, Nikolai Bukharin, Lev Kamenev, Grigory Zinoviev, Karl Radek and Yakov Sverdlov. Fascist propaganda has always lumped together "Bolsheviks" and "Jews." Therefore the appearance of an anti-Semitic book in the greatest Socialist country was confusing to unsophisticated people.

Stalin, like Hitler, annihilated Jews, although he never did this openly. Many Jewish Communists who escaped from Germany to the Soviet Union were turned over to the Gestapo after the signing of the Nazi-Soviet non-aggression pact. During the prewar purges, a large number of Jews were killed in the Siberian concentration camps, supposedly because of their "Zionism." At the same time the famous Jewish theater in Moscow was closed, and Jewish printing and publishing concerns were destroyed.

Little is known about the attitudes of the Stalin bureaucracy toward Jews during World War II. The evacuation of the territories conquered by Germans was planned in a way that made it impossible for Jews to get permission to retreat with the Red Army into the interior. Everyone who tried to escape from the Germans without permission to evacuate was instantly shot. So Russian Jews found

[42] Cf. *The New Leader,* March 16, 1964, which reproduced anti-Semitic cartoons from *Judaism Without Embellishment.*

themselves between two fires. As Georgy Klomov wrote in his book *The Kremlin in Berlin*, translated in Yugoslavia about 10 years ago, several tens of thousands of Jews lost their lives because of that situation in 1941, when the German tanks arrived at Moscow and the evacuation of the city started. Two or three years before Stalin's death, anti-Semitism was in full swing. Only because of the death of the "Wise Leader" did 20 Moscow doctors—Jews—remain with their heads on their shoulders. Once they were accused of "attempting to poison" Soviet leaders; now they live normal lives in Moscow.

A prominent Muscovite in the field of education told me that, although he graduated from high school in 1952 with high honors and received a gold medal, he was not allowed to register at Moscow University because of his Jewish ancestry and had to study in the provinces. He said: "Our greatest tragedy is that we consider ourselves Russians." A rejection on such grounds couldn't happen today.[43] Still, "Jewish jokes" circulate in which, as a rule, "a Communist and a Jew" carry on a conversation and clash with each other: an illogical confrontation on some illogical question.

I had occasion on the first day of my visit to experience Soviet anti-Semitism myself. When at the border station they attached the coach of the Belgrade train to the Soviet train, I went through the whole train several times

---

[43] More recent reports from the Soviet Union indicate that a quota system limiting the number of Jewish students in Soviet institutions of higher learning still exists.

examining the passengers and coaches. As I was passing through the dining car, a passenger sitting at a table said something loudly. But only when I passed him the second time did I realize that his remark was directed at me. The middle-aged man, slightly drunk, remarked: "See, a Jew is taking a walk." I was so astonished by this that I nearly approached him to explain that I was not a Jew, but a Kavkazian through my grandfather, and the son of a White Russian émigré. Fortunately, I did not do this.

THE PSYCHOLOGY
OF HOMO SOVIETICUS

How good it is that all the enthusiasts are dead. Otherwise they would live to see that their work did not move forward one step, that their ideals remained ideals, and that it is not enough to smash the Bastille into pebbles in order to make out of confused prisoners free men.— ALEKSANDR HERZEN

The Soviets have a psychology of their own, typically Soviet. It is a psychology of men who identify themselves with the entire history of the Soviet Union, with all the ideas which set in motion (and sometimes hinder) life in the Soviet Union. In general, one meets such men in the various Soviet delegations, in Intourist, etc., but not every one of the 10 million members of the Soviet Communist

145

Party is a *homo sovieticus,* though there is no doubt that
the percentage of them is greater among Party members.
For one thing membership in the Soviet Communist Party
—an organization deprived of any democratic base, which
unquestioningly carries out orders from the "top" (*verkh-
ushka*)—requires a more or less constabulary character.
There are also weak people who believe all the absurdities
of the top. Until recently, for example, every single leader
in the history of the Union of Soviet Socialist Republics
was eventually found to be a "capitalistic hireling," a
"traitor," a member of one of the numerous "anti-party"
groups, etc.—including, naturally, Stalin himself, who
was guilty of "hostility toward the people."

The first characteristic of *homo sovieticus* is that he
approves and accepts everything that is decided at the
top with complete sincerity. The second characteristic is
a naive and unthinking Jesuitism of the type described
by Dostoevsky in the person of Erkel, one of the minor
characters of *The Possessed*—honest, sensitive, and pleasant in his personal life, but prepared for the greatest
servilities in the name of a "higher Idea." Following
orders was a necessity for this simple little man who constantly, eagerly, subordinated himself to somebody else's
will for the sake of the "universal" and "great" goal. This
was in vain, however, because petty fanatics like Erkel
can in no way understand what it means to serve an idea,
except to relate it to the man who, they believe, embodies
it. Sensitive, tender and good Erkel—yet perhaps he was
the most insensitive of all the murderers preparing to
attack Shatov, without any personal hatred.

The 20th Party Congress brought much that was positive. It broke the thread to which a system had clung psychologically for thirty years. But just as Stalinism was not only Stalin's fault, so the 20th Congress was not able to destroy all those numerous Erkels who could hardly wait to bow in front of some new deity. Stalinism represented a materialization of the psychological needs of millions of Erkels to whom the liberty to make decisions in every instant of their lives is threatening and impossible, and who, thanks to their plebeian spirit, cannot exist without a "master." It is harder to be a subject than an object, to be a personality rather than part of a collective. It is difficult to bear responsibilities and easy to proclaim that man is determined by social history and "laws" of nature.

Homo sovieticus is immature. He possesses a naive ability to believe his own lies, deliberately closing his eyes to everything that negates those lies; lies which are psychological and theoretical justifications of the greatest servilities to a "higher goal." This is the psychology of the average *homo sovieticus*. It would be naive to believe that any tyranny existed merely because of scoundrels. Every tyranny, even the most horrible one, lasts because of the support of its honest fanatics. The scoundrels are rare, and never bring as many evils as the fanatics.

Unfortunately, the Soviet social system itself still favors the development of Erkels. This starts with the nursery songs taught at the schools as part of the compulsory indoctrination in "collective spirit" (that is, the destruction of any individual personality in a child). The problem of how best to collectivize the spirit (beginning with the Pioneer Youth organization) has been frequently discussed in recent times in the Soviet press, amid glorification of conformity with the mass of "the people." (This is the greatest lie—the masses are not people. Pushkin is people, not the impersonal masses.) The indoctrination continues all the way to the *kolkhozes* and factories. Everywhere, discipline is instilled; orders must be executed and all personal initiative suppressed.

True, conditions are better now than they were in 1956–57, and they are still improving. But every new achievement of the progressive forces is paid for with heavy sacrifices and exhausting struggle. Any action not planned from the top, no matter how useful it may be, is still criticized: There is no greater Soviet sin than an unplanned action. This notion leads to unbelievable absurdities. Thus, last year the Soviet newspapers often printed front page articles about the necessity for flower shops in Moscow, arguing that flowers are not "bourgeois" property but are appropriate to the "proletarian relationship" among people. Finally, it was announced that a committee of the Mossoviet would consider the matter. I do not know what the decision was, but the very fact that the issue required grave discussions on the front pages speaks for itself.

In fact, today there is no more conservative society than the Soviet society. The slightest change, even a new kind of tie, song or trouser leg width, provokes great resistance. The 20th Congress fired a significant blow at *homo sovieticus*. The young generation, especially the students, painfully and deeply feel all these absurdities of centralized statism; they are dissatisfied with the slow tempo of liberalization. But this dissatisfaction goes to the other extreme of absurdity. Thus, a student at Moscow University, speaking about lack of respect for the individual in the Soviet Union, angrily cited this as an example: In broadcasting light music a Soviet disc jockey announces the titles of selections only after a few bars have been played, so it is impossible to tape the whole composition without taping the speaker's voice too. Obviously this is simply a case of a broadcasting cliché, yet it is symptomatic that the young man in question considers it interference with the rights of an individual. Robert Rozhdestvensky's verses, *Rodina* ("Native Land") in *Pravda* of December 16, 1962, have become very popular among the youth:

> *We do not want to say any more:*
> *Somebody thinks for us.*
> *We know how that ends.*

Goethe once noted that there was no worse government than paternalism. Unhappily, centuries of imperial autocracy and decades of Stalinism have left the Soviets a terrifying inheritance—limitless paternalism. The "Tsar, Little Father" guides the common man, the child. These ideas subconsciously provide the psychological base for *homo sovieticus*. He has been raised with the "paternal and maternal" fear that the child will be misled, the compulsion to read not what he wants but that which "educates," an instinctive horror of liberalism, a disbelief in man (and all mistrust of others reflects a lack of confidence in oneself), and the conviction that, without paternal care and leadership, he will fail. In answer to my question why all the restaurants close at 10:30 P.M., one boy said to me ironically: "The government is taking care of our health." It seems Tolstoy foresaw something similar to this when he wrote, in his essay "On Education":

"Education, if planned to form people according to definite ideals, is unlawful and untenable. Education damages, it does not improve people. The less a child is spoiled, the less it will be necessary to educate him, and the more freedom he will need. Do not be afraid. Nothing human is damaging to man. You doubt it? Give yourself freely to your emotions, do away with all the conclusions of reason—and the feeling will not trick you. Have trust in its nature."

But Tolstoy wrote in vain. As Lev Shestov says: "Even if the truth could be written in capital letters on every corner, one who was not told to read it wouldn't notice it." It is completely unimaginable to *homo sovieticus*, it is absurd and incredible that someone somewhere in the world could print his own opinions in the newspapers, opinions which do not coincide with those of the "official program" of the community he lives in. It is unimaginable to *homo sovieticus* that someone in power could acknowledge the right of another to make a free decision.

The persuasion that democracy has never existed in any form and never will (for without authoritarian control the world would be destroyed) is so deep that it leads to unbelievable nonsense. Here is one passage from E. Kol'man's book *Is There a God?*.[44] "In the capitalistic states even today scientists who do not believe in God are persecuted. In the United States, the millionaires who govern are spreading throughout the whole world the story of American 'freedom of thought,' but at the same time they persecute and starve those lecturers who teach the truth about the origin of the earth, of life and man. It often happens that scientific works are publicly burned."

Thus American McCarthyism and "witch hunts" are cited to strengthen and help maintain the paternalist-Stalinistic powers of the Soviet land.

The psychology of *homo sovieticus* is strongly plebeian; it lacks spiritual (as opposed to biological or sociological) aristocratic feeling. It is the attitude of a servant in love with his master, and it is evident in all aspects of life: a complete absence of confidence in one's own opinion, a need for leadership and advice from experts. At root, indeed, it is a blind trust in a science which knows better than we do how to sleep with our own wives, how to be friends with our friends, even what we really want in life. The well-known American Marxist Erich Fromm[45] writes:

[44] *Is There a God?* is not actually a book, but a 33-page pamphlet issued by the *Molodaya Gvardiya* publishing outlet in 1958.
[45] Fromm's books have been published in Yugoslavia. Mihajlov quotes from the translation of *Escape From Freedom*.

"One type of curtain of darkness is in an agreement that problems are too complicated for the average individual to understand them. On the contrary, it seems as if many basic conflicting points between the individual and the social order are very simple—so simple, in fact, that everyone should be expected to understand them. To allow these questions to appear so complicated that only one 'expert' can understand them, and even he only in a limited context, means, in fact, often intentionally, to lean toward thwarting man's leaning on his own ability to think about those problems, which are indeed important. An individual feels that he is helplessly caught in the jumbled multitude of facts, and with a pathetic patience, he waits for the experts to discover what he should do, and where he should go."

There is no denying that every time a man transfers the responsibility to someone else for his own behavior, he lightens his own existence. But the punishment is inescapable: "Any jamming into a herd is the result of a lack of talent, regardless of whether it means being faithful to Solovyov or Kant or Marx. Only individuals seek truths, and they break away from anyone who does not like truth enough," wrote Boris Pasternak in his famous novel. And more: "The main misfortune, the root of all evil was the loss of faith in the value of one's own thinking."

The most essential quality of the psyche of *homo sovieticus* is its inner justification for tyrannies and lies: Force is used and lies are told for love, in the same manner that parents act out of love for their children. Never have greater evils been performed than some of those done out of love. It provides the psychological justification for the secret police. In a healthy society, allowing every open and public criticism and opposition, a secret police would be an absurdity. Hence the Soviet fear of public opinion. All the discussions in Soviet magazines and newspapers are more or less skillfully arranged. But the existence of serious problems, about which there is silence, is revealed by the numerous anonymous letters received by the editors of Soviet newspapers (not too long ago, *Komsomolskaya Pravda* attacked the authors of these letters).

Homo sovieticus lacks awareness of the historical past. It is as if the world began only yesterday. All that went on before 1917 is not only utterly unimportant, but uninteresting as well. This mentality is partly medieval, partly Renaissance, partly the product of a philosophy of its own: Enthusiasm for technology, a naive belief that only modern science can bring happiness to mankind, and that it will unquestionably solve all the problems of the human struggle (as soon as it discovers all the natural laws), a deep conviction that all non-Marxist thinkers are either capitalistic hirelings or immoral idiots—all this is accepted by the quite immature mind of *homo sovieticus*. Astonishing, the impersonality of this mind of the "man from the masses," as the great philosopher Ortega y Gasset put it. All are alike, and from the expressions on their faces you can see with whom you are dealing. But I must admit that I have never met such a person among the students, although an Italian student in Moscow told me there are many.

This intellectual "innocence" at first entertains, but later unbearably exhausts. When you learn that the person with whom you are talking is deeply convinced that Ernst Mach and Richard Avenarius are the last great achievements of "bourgeois" philosophy; that in the 20th century, with the exceptions of Henri Barbusse and Louis Aragon, there were no significant French writers; that Bergson and Freud[46] are convinced reactionaries and enemies of the enlightenment (no one knows about Kierkegaard); and when in a conversation with an historian you find out that he has never read Oswald Spengler; when you learn all of this, you fall into despair. The young generation will have to wage a fierce struggle to clear away these spiritually strangling weeds.

On the other hand, no matter how paradoxical it seems, the very same people bow before the West like servants. In fact these are the two sides of a coin, and within the next two or three decades we shall probably witness a repetition of what occurred in the last century, a conflict

[46] In 1963 the Institute of Philosophy of the Soviet Academy of Sciences published (in a tiny edition of only 5,000) a book entitled *Contemporary Psychology in the Capitalist Countries,* co-authored by seven Soviet psychologists. As the very title of the book suggests, it is marked by an outlook ranging from the hostile to the contemptuous; the first sentence in the chapter on Freudianism, for example, reads: "Freudianism is one of the most widespread and reactionary movements in contemporary bourgeois psychology." Nonetheless, the very scope of the book (discussing, often for the first time in Soviet print, such figures as Adler, Jung, Horney, Skinner, and numerous others) gives it a certain significance, and it may be seen as a first halting step back into 20 century psychology.

between the new "Slavophiles" and "Westerners."[47] A very appealing Moscow youth who works for Intourist, Jury Zuev, told me of a dishonest act by a foreign student. He said: "A European should not act that way." A girl talked to me with envy of her boss' traveling occasionally "to Europe." All possible articles from abroad are highly priced, and you are approached on the streets and asked to sell pieces of your clothing. To go on a tour of Europe is an unattainable dream in the Soviet Union. Permission (*putyovka*) is only given to the select.

And what about those people who cannot be characterized as *homo sovieticus?* Once, I had occasion to see a very interesting event in Red Square. My guide, Oleg Merkurov, and I were standing on the street in front of St. Basil's Church intending to take photographs. Suddenly a very shabbily dressed man in his fifties, bent over, with suffering eyes, said in an angry trembling voice to my guide, who had a camera in his hands: "You are taking my picture, too, you swine. Not enough that you already crushed me." Confused, Oleg tried to calm him, but the man waved his hand and went away.

On another occasion, I saw a similar incident in Maxim Gorky Park. In front of the ticket office of a dance hall stood a long line of about 200 people. At one point a man—probably the one in charge—came out of the hall and, addressing the people at the end of the line, told

[47] "Slavophilism" was one of the important schools of 19th century Russian thought which protested Slavic dependence upon the West and advocated Pan-Slavic unity.

them there was no sense in waiting in line when only about 100 meters away there was another hall which was never crowded, where an excellent orchestra under the "Kremlin bandmaster's" direction was playing. Some young people in the line, apparently workers, started to laugh, and one said, "Well, since it is under the direction of the Kremlin, it isn't worth anything." The others in the line, although smiling, turned their heads away from the younger workers.

In Moscow and in Leningrad I was also told about an incident involving a group of students from the Leningrad Technological Institute during the 1956 Hungarian Revolution. The students assembled in front of the former Winter Palace—now the Hermitage—and shouted "Hands off Hungary!" Of course, they vanished from the Institute and from the city.

Homo sovieticus differs from other people in his attitudes toward reality, and, as I have said, it is very easy to recognize him after a few words. No matter what the topic of conversation, whether it be the imperfections of the Moscow city maps (only about a week after my arrival the maps appeared in the kiosks), or the space flights, or the construction of apartment buildings, *homo sovieticus* will always say: "*We* did not print enough city maps, *we* have flown into space, *we* have built. . . ." The common people will say: "*They* have not printed enough maps, *they* have made a flight into space, *they* have built some more apartments. . . ." "We" and "they."

A common man from the countryside is disturbed mostly by the following things:

1. *Retention of the kolkhozniks on the collective farms:* No one can leave the *kolkhoz* without a passport, and the passports are kept by the *kolkhoz* administrators. Since the standard of life on the *kolkhoz* is still on a much lower level than the standard of living of the least paid factory workers, the *kolkhozes* would become uninhabited without strict administrative measures. "Serf laws!" a student said of them to me.

2. *Great variances in salaries:* While an unskilled worker can buy two pairs of men's shoes on his month's pay of about 60 rubles, technical experts and administrative officials, who earn 500–600 rubles per month, can buy two television sets.

3. *The "limited attendance" schools:* After the school reform of 1959, when it was decided that all students would be obliged to work two years in industry or agriculture following graduation from high school, so-called "limited attendance" schools were established. There are four of them in Moscow, they say, and others in large cities. The teaching in these schools is very advanced, and is carried on three different languages at the same time. In theory, only exceptionally talented children are to be admitted to these schools. In fact, however, it is the children of the privileged classes who attend them.

4. *Compulsory Army training of three to four years:* Are people afraid of war? I must admit that I was quite surprised by the complete indifference toward war and toward the conflict with China among those whom I have met. "To live is so boring," one young girl from Leningrad said to me.

The government constantly, and for the most part un-successfully, battles for increased work output. Even at the large establishments which are shown to foreign delegations and at the prominent *kolkhozes,* work is of poor quality and the output is minimal. The Soviet press constantly writes about this, appealing to the conscious-ness of the "builders of Communism." The results are the eternal posters celebrating the "Brigades of Com-munist work," and "the brigades which compete for the title—Brigade of Communist Work." Massive fluctuations in employment have made it necessary to issue passports (they are being issued right now) on which every transfer from one job to another will be noted. These will facilitate control of such labor shifts. Fortunately, the draconic laws dating from before World War II, according to which a worker could have been sent to a camp because of a few absences from work without a valid reason, are not in effect any more. Of course, until the time when the entire economic system is adjusted to deemphasize state control, all those posters, which have been used for 47 years to raise the "working élan of the masses," will be absurdities. The process of trying to do away with planned agriculture is underway right now, but it is only a small beginning.

Despite the declaration of Evtushenko, who said "It is a miracle that after all that went on in our country for decades, our people did not become cynics," I must admit that I was often surprised in my contacts with people at the extent of their cynicism. One student said to me with a sarcastic smile: "Oh, you too want to see Lenin's holy relics." Another one showed me a thick book, *History of the Communist Party of the Soviet Union,* and said: "As you can see, I am preparing for an examination on Lenin's religion." In the same vein, there are numerous jokes about everything and anything. One goes like this: "Of course there will be no war, but we will fight for peace, fight so well that there will not be a stone left standing."

As an answer to the naiveté of the lies, which only the average *sovieticus* can accept, the young respond with fanatical hatred to even a very small lie in their social or private lives. The Soviet press writes about this characteristic trend of the younger generation with a condescending laudatory smile, behind which one feels them thinking, "They're young, foolish." Unconsciously I recall Pasternak: "It is impossible to keep quiet from day to day about what one is thinking and feeling without serious consequences to one's health. It is impossible to make believe that one is happy about something that brings unhappiness. Our nervous system is not a mere phrase; it is not imaginary." (*Doctor Zhivago.*)

A double standard and a degree of insincerity are part of the everyday life of the Soviet man, generally speaking. Even the basic double standards, like those of Stalin and Stalinism, are criticized, but the majority of the ideas which still govern the life and thought of the country were created by Stalin, from Socialist Realism to the *kolkhoz.* And it is obvious that the Soviet Union will have to de-Stalinize itself in much greater measure than it is doing now, or else the wheel of history will come around again to Stalinism, and the whole period from 1956 will be proclaimed the work of "traitors."

More energetic de-Stalinization is hardly likely, however, despite the fact that Khrushchev[48] himself enjoys great popularity among the people. Some still consider him too much of a Stalinist and recall his activities during Stalin's era. It was Khrushchev himself, together with Ezhov, who purged the Ukraine. Among those executed in that purge was the Secretary of the Central Committee of the Ukraine, Stanislav Kosior, whom Khrushchev rehabilitated so wholeheartedly. Some—the older type of *homo sovieticus*—think that Khrushchev is hurting "the cause of Communism." There are outright Stalinists, still in great number, even among the younger generation between the age of 20–25. One 20-year-old Moscow girl told me: "Stalin was right to butcher them. He was butchering bastards!"

A completely apolitical, typically middle-class intelligentsia, or, more correctly, semi-intelligentsia is also emerging—an army of technicians interested only in material gain. Probably these technical and technocratic groups will play a more and more important role in the life of the Soviet Union in the near future. Khrushchev was appealing precisely to them when he spoke of raising the standard of living to a higher level. Yet it is a fact, no matter how paradoxical, that the common Russian people do not consider material poverty the greatest mis-

[48] It should again be pointed out that when *Moscow Summer 1964* was written, of course, Khrushchev was still in power.

fortune, even though their living standard is still very low (about 40 per cent lower than in Yugoslavia).

Let us recall Dostoevsky's words: "Build a palace. Use marble, pictures, gold, birds of paradise, hanging gardens, everything that exists. . . . And now enter it. Perhaps you will not want to leave it ever. Maybe, indeed, you won't come out. There is plenty of everything. Why look for black bread when you have white? But suddenly, let's suppose, someone builds a fence around your palace and tells you: Everything is yours, enjoy yourself, but you will not be allowed to leave. You may be sure that at that same instant you will want to leave your paradise and go beyond the fence. And more than that, all this luxury, all this wealth will merely increase your suffering. Precisely this luxury will hurt you. . . . For there is one thing missing: 'Freedom.' "

The young people especially do not see any great misfortune in the low standard of living because they are striving to climb Calvary for the sake of a great idea which does not exist any longer. Pavel Korchagin[49] was fighting for a "Paradise on earth," not for a "high standard of living." And precisely because of this lack of "spiritual sustenance" the various religious sects flourish. The gov-

[49] Pavel Korchagin is the hero of Nikolai Ostrovsky's 1932 proletarian novel *How the Steel Was Tempered*. Ostrovsky, who died in 1936, was blind and partially paralyzed during most of his mature years, and he is one of the more sympathetic and honorable practitioners of that dubious Soviet genre. Actually, his novel as it first appeared was not without literary interest; most of its better features were preened out subsequently, making *How the Steel Was Tempered* a model of Socialist Realism.

ernment is trying to direct the minds of young people toward the development of Siberia and the conquest of space, but without much success. Perhaps only the threat of China will mobilize the spiritual forces of the Russian people. However, no one really feels this threat as yet.

CONCLUSIONS
AND PERSPECTIVES

Various religions exist because people believe in others and not in themselves. I myself trusted other people and wandered as if in a wilderness. . . . Everyone should believe in his own spirit, and all will be united. Let everyone believe in himself, and all will be one.—LEO TOLSTOY, *Resurrection*

I was inclined towards revolution, but now I believe that nothing can be achieved by force.—BORIS PASTERNAK, *Doctor Zhivago*

The Soviet Union finds itself on the verge of great changes. The year 1956 was only the first wave. The destiny not only of mankind but of all life on earth depends greatly on what is going on today in the Soviet Union. Therefore, everything that is happening in this important country attracts the attention of the world.

But all that has happened in the Soviet Union shows that the solution to man's crisis is not to be found in the political, social or economic spheres. It lies much deeper, in the existential, universal crisis of the personality, in the metaphysical depths of human beings. We must search in the writings of religious thinkers on the loss of God, and in the Marxist texts on human estrangement, which is to say, alienation—no less pronounced in a totalitarian society where mankind is made into a collective by force than it is in the capitalist world. On the one hand, there are a multitude of disconnected individuals with no internal spiritual stays. On the other, there is the rigidly ordered society in which individuals must withdraw into themselves even more—Kafka's world: A machine in motion has no more life in it than a motionless object!

The real paradox lies in the fact that although man longs to come out of his loneliness, any forceful joining together only prevents this. De-Stalinization, or more precisely, the smashing of the machine, opens the way to an organic society—that is, to the free unification of people. The means is not contract but contact. Therefore, Stalinism is not only a political, but above all an existential, a religious problem. It is like Hitlerism (from which it got its rightful label, "cult"). The very existence of the Soviet Union has refuted all the theories which teach that a society's economic base and development of productive forces can condition its ideology. For nearly half a century, Soviet ideology, or the so-called super-structure, has been the decisive factor in Soviet social and economic relations.

Men never were moved to go to war by a desire for economic welfare, but only by a longing for "spiritual sustenance." And this is true not merely of the early Christians but of the Russian revolutionaries as well—they died for "justice over the entire earth," rather than for a high standard of living. Nazis, conquering the world, dying on the fronts of Europe and Africa, were also there not because of the economic gains they expected after the war, but because of the idea of the "One-Thousand-Year Reich."

The Soviet Union and the rest of the world find themselves at a significant crossroads. The old dominant idea which motivated men, the idea of an "earthly paradise," does not work any more. This is not because it is un-realizable; quite the contrary. For although the contours of the economically and socially just society can already be perceived in many ways, it is being realized that this alone does not give spiritual sustenance. The lawfully ordered welfare society makes sense only if it serves as a means to something and not as an end in itself.

Out of this grows spiritual confusion. The heretofore connective tissue (if not for the entire Soviet nation, then at least for the fanatics of the hierarchy) has disintegrated. There remains now only one goal—attaining a high standard of living. Undoubtedly, the numerous measures being enacted in the Soviet Union to decentralize agriculture and other sectors of the economy will succeed in attaining that sooner or later. However, just at that point the essential problems will arise—and then what? For man will never be satisfied with the idea that he is born in this cosmos and "that's all," that his only aim in life is to live well. Here is the weakness of Khrushchev's ideology. There can be no doubt that a new revolution is coming, one which Mayakovsky predicted: a revolution in spiritual spheres. Surely Marxism will remain permanently as a science about *society*, but new spiritual movements will concern themselves with the human soul. The threat from the Asiatic nations, indeed, hastens the formation of the new ideology. In my opinion, it will be some sort of assertive individualism (whether "socialistic" or "Christian" is irrelevant). And classical Russian philosophy (Solovyov, Shestov, Berdyaev) will play a very important role in all this. I consider that Spengler was right in a way, regarding the great future of Russia and its ideology.

However, there is so much preventing the abolition of the old structure. Let us examine who and what. In 1933, Nikolai Berdyaev in his famous work *The Sources and Meaning of Russian Communism* wrote: "This new Soviet bureaucracy is stronger than the Tsarist bureaucracy, it is a new privileged class, which can ferociously exploit the masses. This is happening."

In my opinion, this does not hold true today to the same degree. From 1956 on, changes occurred in many respects in the power structure, and that these changes are still going on is evident from the anti-Stalinist clean-up (*chistka*) which is taking place right now, according to what is being written everywhere in the European press.

The process of de-Stalinization has advanced quite far. Today a completely new social class is being formed. The Party and State bureaucracy are little by little being squeezed out by this new class, this technocratic intelligentsia. Knowledge is becoming power. All the future conflicts within the Soviet Union, with the onset of this "third revolution," will be directed not so much against the bureaucracy as against the technocracy. Substitution of intellectual power for political power, however, does not change or solve anything at all. As Berdyaev says: "Power is possible only over an object, not over a subject." Alienation is not solved until all kinds of authority are eliminated. Just as the abolition of individual economic power (over goods and production) did not abolish power, so the abolition of political power will not abolish the intellectual power of technocracy. And authority is the very cause of alienation, preventing true contact between people. The struggle against authority automatically brings in its wake the struggle against "Reason" (*ratio*), i.e., against science and discovery as the goals of man's earthly life.

The young Ehrenburg said it very nicely in *Julio Jurenito* in 1921: "A stick will always stay a stick, regardless of whose hand holds it. It would be very hard for it to become a mandolin or a Japanese fan. Power without a jail is a debased and uneasy notion, something like a cat with its claws cut. . . . Not just years will pass, but epochs and centuries before the world grasps that it is not a question of who happens to be holding the stick now, but rather a question of the stick itself; not of making it change hands, but of beginning to break it."

This means that only the destruction of all power will open the door to spiritual unity for mankind. It is impossible (fortunately) to force man to be good. Man alone wants to come out of his loneliness, but any kind of force prevents him from doing this. As one Russian proverb says: "One is not driven into Heaven with a club." De-Stalinization seemingly creates the possibility for the renewed *embourgeoisement* of the Soviet Union, but only seemingly, because this is only one essential stage toward a new kind of unity, this time without coercion.

The Soviet Union at this moment is making an exit from Asia, attaching itself to Europe, and moving toward democracy. Everything that accelerates this movement plays a positive role. So very much has to be rehabilitated—the value of free thought, the value of authentic democracy, the lasting value of certain basic truths in all domains of human life, the abolition of all secrecy, and more. The Soviet press is rapidly improving, but until there are independent media, there will be no free press, and thus no public opinion.

Many changes await the Soviet Union, a land culturally two decades behind Western Europe. These include revision of the myth of the October Revolution (here *The Russian Revolution* by Rosa Luxemburg will play an important role, because it was, in fact, Lenin who opened the path for Stalin, as Ivan Karamazov dragged the action of Smerdyakov after him); a critical approach to the "myth of science"; the destruction of the myth of the usefulness of every type of labor (for work and creativity stand in the same relation as prostitution and love); and the reevaluation of Russian literature and Russian philosophy. The last two processes have already begun. The changes will be great and far-reaching. The more revolutionary among the younger generation will carry them out, because, as Georg Lukacs says in his *History and Class Consciousness:* "The spirit of revolution is not determined by the radicalism of its aims, nor by the type of means which are employed in the struggle. The spirit of revolution is a totality, a wholeness brought to bear on every act of living." From that point of view, we could say that Pasternak is more revolutionary than many of those who have attacked him. Naturally, he himself did not realize this, and identified revolution with force.

In this great turn of events in the Soviet Union, Yugoslavia can again play an important role, just as it did in 1948.

BIOGRAPHICAL
INFORMATION

BIOGRAPHICAL INFORMATION

Mihajlov's essay is a veritable forest of names, therefore it simply was not practical to supply additional biographical data, titles of available English translations, etc. within the text proper. And even as a separate section, the compilation of the biographies presented serious problems: should every name mentioned be included? should only Russians be listed? and, if so, what about world-famous Russians (Tolstoy, Dostoevsky) and comparatively little-known non-Russians (Ernst Bloch, Lucien Goldmann)? The Editor's decision was to keep the biographical notes primarily Russian and literary, since that, after all, is the substance of *Moscow Summer*. An important sub-grouping is that of Russian philosophy, another subject discussed at considerable length by Mihajlov. Certain foreigners and certain political figures have been admitted when it seemed that this might be necessary and helpful to a significant number of readers, and certain Russians have been excluded when they are either too well known or too insignificant. Beyond that, some four or five names dropped *en passant* by Mihajlov refused to yield any biographical data at all—an occupational hazard of contemporary Soviet studies.

These notes, then, are intended to provide information and suggested further reading on individual writers and philosophers who might be of interest to particular readers. Beyond that, it is hoped that their perusal can make the reading of *Moscow Summer* more interesting and rewarding to the non-specialist reader.

Bella AKHMADULINA (1936–   ). The former wife of poet Evgeny Evtushenko and the present wife of writer Yury Nagibin, Akhmadulina is the most outstanding young Soviet poetess writing today, or, some would even say, the most outstanding young Soviet poet regardless of sex. For a long time Akhmadulina was unable to print her poems, and she finally gained membership in the Writers' Union, through a strategem of friends, as a trans-

lator. Her first book of poems, *A String*, was published in 1962, and she has since published several long poems in literary journals. Only one short poem by Akhmadulina has been translated into English, and it appeared in *Encounter* (April, 1963) and subsequently in the anthology *Halfway to the Moon* (Holt, Rinehart & Winston, 1965).

Anna AKHMATOVA (1888–   ). Although she is mentioned only in passing in Mihajlov's essay, Akhmatova, who lives in Leningrad, is widely considered to be Russia's greatest living poet. Long before the 1917 Revolution, Akhmatova was recognized as one of the leading poets in the Acmeist movement; she also published several books of poetry after 1917, but then she began to encounter Party hostility, culminating in a vicious campaign against her in 1946. Nevertheless, it is not true, as is often claimed, that Akhmatova is a "pre-revolutionary poet" who has produced little in modern times, for an ever-increasing number of her poems, written in an entirely fresh manner, have been appearing both in Russia and abroad. Translations of her poetry are available in the *Penguin Book of Russian Verse* (1962), *Tri-Quarterly* (Spring, 1965), and *The Atlantic* (October, 1964).

Samuil ALYOSHIN (?). The author of five plays dealing with problems of contemporary Soviet life, several of which have enjoyed great popularity. *The Hospital Ward*, the play discussed by Mihajlov, has not been translated into English, but another Alyoshin play, *Alone* (1956), is available in the paperback *Year of Protest: 1956* (Vintage, 1961). Alyoshin's plays are of greater sociological than artistic interest.

Leonid ANDREEV (1871–1919). Andreev was a very successful pre-revolutionary popularizer of Symbolist themes. His writings tend to be shallow and by now have lost almost all of the enormous popularity they once enjoyed, but several of his plays demonstrate true dramatic mastery—one of the best of them *He Who Gets Slapped* (1914) is available in the paperback *20th Century Russian Drama* (Bantam, 1963).

Pavel ANTOKOL'SKY (1896–   ). Antokol'sky is not a major figure, but he is a poet of talent whose poems are widely read in the Soviet Union. In his role as one of the editors of the yearly *Day of Poetry* volumes, Antokol'sky has given great aid to many younger poets, and he was, in fact, the editor responsible for the publication of Bella Akhmadulina's first book of poems. Translations of two of Antokol'sky's poems may be found in the *Penguin Book of Russian Verse* (Penguin, 1962).

Isaac BABEL (1894–1941). Babel is a leading Soviet short story writer and playwright defined rather nicely by Stanley Edgar Hyman as "the foremost minor writer of the 20th century." He died in a Soviet concentration camp. English translations of Babel include *Collected Stories* (Meridian, 1955) and *The Lonely Years* (Farrar, Straus & Giroux, 1964).

Demyan BEDNY (1883–1945). Bedny—his real name was Efimy Pridvorov—is the author of "proletarian" tales and poems, all unspeakably wretched. At one time he was hailed as a "giant" of Soviet literature, and the 1930 Soviet *Literary Encyclopedia* featured a full-page portrait of him.

Vissarion BELINSKY (1811–1848). Belinsky is the father of the socially conscious, utilitarian outlook in Russian literary criticism which demands "realism" and "social responsibility" above all in literature. He has become a patron saint of the official canon of Socialist Realism, which is the sense behind Viktor Shklovsky's statement, quoted by Mihajlov, that "I'll crush Belinsky with the legs of my writing desk."

Andrei BELY (1880–1934). Bely (Boris Bugaev) was one of the leading Russian Symbolist poets and writers, but, even more important perhaps, his modernistic, ornamental prose influenced a whole generation of early Soviet writers. His most important novel, *St. Petersburg* (1913–16), has been translated into English (Grove, 1960).

Nikolai BERDYAEV (1874–1948). Berdyaev is one of the outstanding Russian philosophers of this century. In his

youth he was arrested as a Marxist Socialist, but subsequently he became a religious thinker for which, ironically, he was expelled by the Bolsheviks from Russia in 1922. Berdyaev believed that man does have free will (by virtue of which God is not omnipotent), but that salvation cannot be attained individually but only through a communality of belief. After he left Russia, Berdyaev lived in Paris where he headed the important YMCA Russian publishing house. Almost all of his many books have been translated into English.

Ernst BLOCH (1885–   ). Bloch is a prominent German philosopher and "Marxist revisionist," best known for his *The Spirit of Utopia* (1923)

Yury BONDARYOV (1924–   ). The majority of Bondaryov's novels and stories are concerned with war themes. His most important novel, *Silence*, recently appeared in a British translation published by Chapman & Hall.

Nikolai BUKHARIN (1888–1938). Bukharin was a leading Communist theoretician who at first allied himself with Stalin, but, between 1929 and 1934, fell from favor. He was tried for "treason" in 1938 and executed. He was not, as Mihajlov states, a Jew.

Sergei BULGAKOV (1871–1944). Bulgakov was a leading Russian Orthodox philosopher who wrote on Karl Marx "as a religious type" and the history of Russian idealism. His book *The Orthodox Church* has been translated into English (NY, 1935).

Nikolai CHERNYSHEVSKY (1828–1889). Chernyshevsky was an important early Populist polemicist and critic. In 1863 he published a utopian novel *What Is To Be Done* (NY, 1959), and in the same year he was banished to Siberia. Chernyshevsky is the object of an extended and hilarious satire in Vladimir Nabokov's novel *The Gift*.

Nikolai CHUKOVSKY (1904–   ). Chukovsky, son of the famed critic and children's writer Kornei Chukovsky, is the author of some Socialist Realist fiction, but also of some excellent and colorful stories, one of which, *The Tramp,* has been translated in the paperback *Great Soviet*

Short Stories (Dell, 1962). Chukovsky's forthcoming memoirs, segments of which have appeared in *Moskva* and *Day of Poetry,* are being awaited with great anticipation.

Nikolai DANILEVSKY (1822–1885). Danilevsky was an important 19th century Russian Darwinist and advocate of Pan-Slavism. His most famous works are *Darwinism* and *Russian and Europe.*

Vladimir DUDINTSEV (1918–   ). Dudintsev achieved world-wide fame with his 1956 novel *Not By Bread Alone* (Dutton, 1957) which became a primary document in the struggle for liberalization within the Soviet Union. He also has written a much shorter work *A New Year's Tale*

(Dutton, 1960) which has much greater artistic merit although it aspires to greater depth than it can in fact claim.

Ilya EHRENBURG (1891–   ). Ehrenburg made his first appearance in literature as a poet, prior to 1917. From 1921 until 1937 he lived abroad, returning to Russia to become one of Stalin's foremost propagandists, although now he is counted in the "liberal" camp. Ehrenburg's best novel, *Julio Jurenito,* is available in English (Philadelphia, 1964), and his memoirs *People, Years, Life* have been translated into English in three volumes and much overpraised.

Vladimir ERMILOV (1904–   ). Ermilov is one of the most reactionary of Soviet literary publicists, credited by many with the denunciation and imprisonment of scores of writers during the Stalinist purges. From 1928–1934 Ermilov was Secretary of the Russian Association of Proletarian Writers.

Vladimir ERN (1881–1915). A minor Russian philosopher in the tradition of Vladimir Solovyov, Ern is best known for his book about the first Russian philosopher, Skovoroda, written in 1912.

Sergei ESENIN (1895–1925). A poet of notoriously bohemian inclination (vividly described in Anatoly Mariengof's *A Novel With No Nonsense* [1928], which has unfortunately never been translated into English), Esenin was married to the American dancer Isadora Duncan and, in 1925, committed suicide, before which he wrote a poem with blood from his own wrists. Esenin is a lyric poet of great talent who is once again being recognized and widely published in the Soviet Union; there are, however, no adequate translations of Esenin in English. Esenin's son, Aleksandr Esenin-Volpin, is the author of some rather pathetic and vitriolic "protest poetry" which was smuggled to the West, as a result of which Esenin-Volpin was confined in a mental institution by the Soviet authorities. Less noticed but more clearly a writer is Esenin's daughter, Tatyana Esenina, who in 1962 published a novella entitled *Zhenya, Wonder of the 20th Century*, a hilarious satire about the mishaps which occur when a genuine "positive hero" appears.

Evgeny EVTUSHENKO (1933–   ). Evtushenko is a major Soviet poetaster who has won renown in the West and (to a lesser degree because, after all, they understand Russian there) in the Soviet Union on the basis of some very outspoken and noble political verses, among them *Winter Station* and *Babi Yar*. In 1963 he was criticized by the Khrushchev government for publishing his *Precocious Autobiography* abroad in *L'Express*.

Aleksandr FADEEV (1901–1956). Fadeev was the author of one of the best novels of romantic heroism in early Soviet literature, *The Rout* (first translated into English as *The Nineteen* in 1929, and more recently as *The Rout* by the Moscow Foreign Languages Publishing House in 1957), but he soon gave his talent over to the Party machinery, in which he played a not too admirable role. Fadeev committed suicide in 1956, supposedly as a result of remorse over his actions during the years of Stalinism.

Georges FLOROVSKY (1893–   ). Father Florovsky is an émigré priest and historian of medieval Christianity who has taught at numerous American universities.

Simon FRANK (1877–1950). Simon Frank is an important Russian émigré thinker who is the author of *Reality and*

Man and *The Bases of Marxism*. One of his books, *God With Us—Three Meditations,* has been translated into English (London, 1946).

Nikolai FYODOROV (1828–1903). Fyodorov lived as a recluse and is even today little known, although Tolstoy said: "I am proud to live in the same century with such a man." Selections from his essays are in *Russian Philosophy* (Quadrangle, 1965).

Ilya GLAZUNOV (?). Glazunov is one of the most promising young Soviet painters. Even though his manner is scarcely "modern"—on the contrary, he seems to concentrate on ancient Russian themes—Glazunov has been the object of official displeasure and has had to devote much of his time to doing book illustrations.

Lucien GOLDMANN (1913–   ). Goldmann's chief interest for Mihajlov is probably his *Études sur la pensée dialectique et son histoire*. In English Goldmann, the author of many books, is represented by *The Hidden God— A Study of Tragic Vision in Pascal and Racine* (London, 1964).

Yakov GOLOSOVKER (?). The author of the single small book discussed by Mihajlov, *Dostoevsky and Kant—A Reader's Thoughts on The Brothers Karamazov and Kant's Critique of Pure Reason,* published in 1963. There is, by the way, no clear link between Kant and Dostoevsky apart from the inclusion of Kant's name in a long list of books which Dostoevsky, writing from Siberia, asked his brother to send him. It is doubtful that he did.

Igor GOLOSOVSKY (1927–   ). Golosovsky is a minor Soviet writer and playwright, the author of such stories as *Whom to Believe* and *The Crimson Stone*.

Oles GONCHAR (1918–   ). Gonchar is a Ukrainian writer who was awarded a Lenin Prize for his novel *Tronka* (1963). His novels and stories have been widely translated into many languages by the official Soviet foreign publishing outlet, but no independent publisher has been moved to print them.

A. V. GORBATOV (1892–   ). Gorbatov is a retired Soviet general whose memoirs, *Years and Wars,* caused somewhat of a sensation by their outspokenness when they appeared in the Soviet journal *Novy Mir* (March–May, 1964). They were published in English under the title *Years Off My Life* (Norton, 1965).

Maxim GORKY (1868–1936). Considered one of the primary pillars of Soviet fiction, Gorky's outstanding works, the play *The Lower Depths* and his *Autobiography,* are pre-revolutionary. Although his complete works contain some of the most boring stories and novels ever written in Russian ("When I have nothing to do, I don't read Gorky," a Russian scholar is said to have quipped), Gorky enjoys almost universal respect both in Russia and abroad for his vital role in saving the lives of many writers in times of both famine and of mass arrests. The circumstances of his death are still mysterious, and it is probable that he was poisoned on Stalin's orders.

Daniil GRANIN (1919–   ). Granin is a prolific Party writer. In 1952 he published a book of stories about the builders of the Soviet Kuibyshev power station; in 1962 he published a book of stories about the builders of Communism in Cuba.

Apollon GRIGOREV (1822–1864). Grigorev was an important thinker, literary critic, and poet, who brilliantly represented the (minority) position against the social obligation of Russian literature in the 19th century. "Only literary rot," he once wrote, "has served, serves, and will continue to serve the public." Happily, Grigorev's fascinating *My Literary and Moral Wanderings* is available in a paperback translation (Dutton, 1962).

Aleksandr GRIN (1880–1932). Grin—his real name was Grinevsky—is one of the most popular Soviet authors owing to the colorful nature of his fantasy, which is conspicuously lacking in Socialist Realist fiction. Among his works are *The Golden Chain, Crimson Sails, Road to Nowhere.* Most of his best stories, such as *The Rat Catcher,* have not been translated, but one story is available in English in the paperback *Dissonant Voices in Soviet Literature* (Colophon, 1965).

Nikolai GUDZY (1887–   ). Professor Gudzy has been one of the most productive Soviet pedagogues who has compiled the standard anthology and written the standard history of ancient Russian literature, in addition to studies on Tolstoy and 18th century Russian realism.

Nikolai GUMILYOV (1886–1921). Gumilyov, who was shot in 1921, was one of the first and foremost casualties in the Soviet reign of terror. Primarily a poet, Gumilyov also wrote stories, plays, and poetry criticism. Owing to the manner in which he died, Gumilyov has been a source of particular embarrassment to the Soviet government, and for many years his name was completely absent from

literary histories, although it has now begun to appear and his poetry is once again being printed. Seven Gumilyov poems have been translated in the *Penguin Book of Russian Verse* (Penguin, 1962).

Mikhail Gus (?). Gus, a young Soviet scholar, has published two books, *Gogol and Nikolai's Russia* (1957) and *The Ideas and Images of Dostoevsky* (1962).

Aleksandr HERZEN (1812–1870). Herzen was a Russian revolutionary thinker who spent much of his mature life in exile in England, where he edited a Russian language paper, *The Bell,* which was smuggled into Russia and exerted an important influence there. He is best known for *The Past and Thoughts,* an autobiographical portrayal of Russian intellectual life in the 1840s.

Leonid ILICHYOV (1907–   ). During Khrushchev's reign Ilichyov was the chief ideological watchdog over the arts, a post he has since relinquished. Ilichyov enjoyed no noticeable popularity among Soviet writers many of whom, in conversation, would affect to make him an "unperson": 'What's his name?" ("*Kak yevó zavoót?*").

Ivan IL'IN (1882–1954). Il'in was an important Russian émigré philosopher and critic. He is the author of two two-volume studies, *Axioms of the Religious Experience* and *Hegel's Philosophy as Instruction on the Concreteness of God and Man*, and a single volume study *On the Opposition of Evil by Force*. In addition Il'in is the author of *On Darkness and Enlightenment*, a study of three émigré writers—Bunin, Remizov, and Shmelyov.

Yury KAZAKOV (1927–   ). Kazakov has published six collections of short stories and is widely considered to be one of the most promising young Russian prose writers. A book of Kazakov's stories has been published in English, *Going to Town* (Houghton, 1964), and three of his stories are in *Pages from Tarusa* (Little, Brown, 1964). At present Kazakov is said to be at work on his first novel.

Rimma KAZAKOVA (1932–   ). Rimma Kazakova's books of poetry include *We'll Meet in the East* and *The Place Where You Are;* in 1964 a volume of her selected poems appeared. The only available Kazakova poems in English are three very poor translations in the official Soviet English-language magazine *Soviet Literature* (March, 1963).

Velemir KHLEBNIKOV (1885–1922). Khlebnikov was one of the leading Russian Futurist poets whose "trans-sense" language makes him one of the most daring and difficult of modern Russian poets. A small collection of his poetry was published in the Soviet Union in 1960 (the first in twenty years), and his work enjoys great popularity among certain young Soviet poets. English translations of two of Khlebnikov's short poems may be found in the *Penguin Book of Russian Verse* (Penguin, 1962).

Vsevolod KOCHETOV (1912–   ). Kochetov, editor of the journal *Oktyabr,* is the leader of the neo-Stalinoid camp in Soviet literature. The titles of some of his books are quite self-explanatory; they are: *Youth Is With Us, Under the Skies of the Motherland, The People's Arms,* and *Secretary of the Obkom.*

Boris LAVRENYOV (1892–   ). As a youth Lavrenyov was connected with the Futurist group of poets, but he switched to prose and wrote some of the most colorful stories which deal with the Revolution. His work should be better known in the West where he is known only as the author of *The Forty-First,* a rather weak story which was made into a widely shown Soviet film.

Leonid LEONOV (1899–   ). Leonov is one of the foremost living Soviet writers. During his lifetime he has covered almost the full spectrum from modernism to Socialist Realism. Leonov's most important work from an artistic point of view is a novel of his early years, *The Thief,* which is available in a paperback translation (Vin-

tage, 1960), and his first short stories, the best of which, *The Wooden Queen,* has been translated in the paperback *Great Soviet Short Stories* (Dell, 1962).

Konstantin LEONT'EV (1831–1891). Leont'ev was an important Russian philosopher and novelist with extremely reactionary political views. One essay appears in *Russian Philosophy* (Quadrangle, 1965). Berdyaev's book, *Leontev,* is available (London, 1940).

Vil' LIPATOV (?). A young Siberian writer and critic whose works include *The Six* (1958), *Wild Mint* (1960), and *The Death of Igor Suzin* (1963).

Nikolai LOSSKY (1870–1965). Lossky, an extremely productive Russian émigré philosopher and scholar, wrote such books as *A History of Russian Philosophy* (International Universities Press, 1951), *Dialectical Materialism in the USSR,* and *Freedom of Will* (London, 1932).

György LUKÁCS (1885–   ). Lukács, a Hungarian, is one of the foremost living Marxist critics, and one of the few living critics whose works are published widely in both the East and the West. English translations of Lukács' books include *The Historical Novel* (Beacon, 1963), *Studies in European Realism* (Grosset, 1964), and *The Meaning of Contemporary Realism* (London, 1963).

Anatoly LUNACHARSKY (1875–1933). Lunacharsky was a Communist critic of great intellectual gifts who wrote widely on 19th century Russian lierature, the Russian theater, and literary theory. He also wrote several plays which are, however, of less interest than his polemical, class-oriented criticism.

Kasimir MALEVICH (1878–1935). Malevich was an early Russian modernist painter whose radical theory of "Suprematism" limited the painter to triangles, squares, and other geometric figures, an approach which ultimately proved too confining. Malevich is best known for his *White on White* (1918), depicting a white square on a white background, which hangs in the Museum of Modern Art in New York.

Osip MANDELSTAM (1891–1943?). Mandelstam is an eminent Russian poet whose books include *The Stone* (1913), *Tristia* (1922) and *The Noise of Time* (1925). When Mandelstam, a true eccentric, was arrested and sent to Siberia, he developed a serious nervous disorder and suffered from the belief that he was going to be shot every day at six. The precise time, place, and manner of his actual death are still not known. Ten of his poems have been translated in the *Penguin Book of Russian Verse* (Penguin, 1962).

Samuil MARSHAK (1887–1964). Marshak was a distinguished Soviet children's poet and translator of Blake, Wordsworth, and Burns.

Leonid MARTYNOV (1905–   ). Although for many years he lived in great poverty and was unable to print his poetry, Martynov is today one of Russia's most widely respected older poets. There are almost no English translations of Martynov's poetry, but several fragments have

been translated in a survey article on modern Soviet poetry which appeared in the *Kenyon Review* (Summer, 1964).

Novella MATVEEVA (?). A talented poetess who has published two books of poetry, *Lyrics* (1961) and *The Little Ship* (1963); in addition, her poetry has appeared in *Day of Poetry, Izvestia,* and the journals *Novy Mir* and *Youth,* and a small booklet of selected poems appeared in 1964. In her poetry Matveeva seems to be under the influence

of Evgeny Vinokurov who, in fact, wrote the foreword to one of her collections. There have been no translations of Matveeva.

Vladimir MAYAKOVSKY (1893–1930). Mayakovsky was a bombastic and brilliant poet who took the 1917 Revolu-

tion as his personal banner and, when it had become tattered, he shot himself in 1930—as the official Communist line goes—"for personal reasons." A good selection of his poems and his 1928 play *The Bedbug* are available in an excellent paperback collection *The Bedbug and Selected Poetry* (Meridian, 1960).

Dmitri MEREZHKOVSKY (1865–1941). Merezhkovsky was a popular and influential but minor novelist and poet of the Russian Symbolist movement. He was a violent critic of tsarism, but after 1917 he went into exile and became even more violently anti-Soviet, even welcoming Hitler's invasion of Russia.

Vsevolod MEYERHOL'D (1874–1942). Meyerhol'd began his career as a student of Stanislavsky but became famous for his highly stylized productions of Symbolist plays by poets such as Aleksandr Blok and Fyodor Sologub. After 1917 Meyerhol'd remained active in the Soviet theater and produced plays by Mayakovsky, Erdman, Gogol, Sel'vinsky, and others. He was arrested in 1939 and died in a Stalinist concentration camp. A collection of Meyerhol'd's dramatic theories has been translated in *Pages from Tarusa* (Little, Brown, 1964).

Boris MIKHAILOVSKY (?). Mikhailovsky is a professor at Moscow University and a member of the Soviet Academy of Sciences. He was entrusted with the task of writing on the "decadent" Russian writers for the multi-volume Soviet *Literary Encyclopedia* in the 1930's, and, although he always passed negative judgment, he still managed to write on them at some length and with some sympathy. In addition to his history of Russian literature from 1900–1917, *Russian Literature of the Twentieth Century*, Prof. Mikhailovsky has also written on ancient Russian art.

Konstantin MOCHUL'SKY (1892–1948). Mochul'sky, the foremost Russian émigré critic and literary historian, wrote books on Aleksandr Blok, Andrei Bely, Dostoevsky, Valery Briusov, Gogol, and Vladimir Solovyov. His study of Dostoevsky has recently been published in an English translation by the Princeton University Press.

Yuna MORITS (1937–   ). One of the youngest of the new Russian poets, Yuna Morits has already published two books of verse, *Conversation on Happiness* and *The Cape of Desires*. Most of her poems have appeared in the journal *Youth* whose editor has expressed confidence in her future artistic development.

Emmanuel MOUNIER (1905–1950). Mounier was a positivist Christian philosopher who wrote extensively on problems of engagement and alienation. Among his books are *Existentialist Philosophies* (London, 1951), and *Personalism* (Verry, Mystic Conn., 1952).

Yury NAGIBIN (1920–   ). Nagibin is the author of several books of short stories. His stories, usually set in the countryside, are good-hearted and moving and have won high praise from some critics, although others have questioned their depth. One of Nagibin's better stories, *The Echo*, has been translated in the anthology *The New Writing in Russia* (University of Michigan, 1964).

Viktor NEKRASOV (1911–   ). Nekrasov won a Stalin Prize in 1947 for his book *In the Trenches of Stalingrad*. In more recent times he drew notice with his story *Kira Georgievna* (Pantheon, 1962) describing what happens to a man who has just returned from a concentration camp. Nekrasov was personally denounced by Khrushchev for his *On Both Sides of the Ocean* (Holt, Rinehart & Winston, 1964), a favorable account of his trip to America. What makes this incident even sadder is the fact that, as Walter Kauffmann pointed out in the *New York Review of Books*, Nekrasov's travelogue is both shallow and banal.

Sergei NIKITIN (1926–   ). Nikitin is the author of seven collections of short stories including *Autumn, Autumn, One's Own House,* and *On a Sleepless Night.*

Pavel NILIN (1908–   ). Nilin is the author of a Siberian detective novel, *Cruelty,* which has been translated into English under the title *Comrade Venka* (Simon & Schuster, 1959).

Bulat OKUDZHAVA (1924–   ). Okudzhava is of Ar-

menian and Georgian descent, although he speaks neither language. Until 1956 he worked as a schoolteacher. His poetry books include *Islands* and, most recently, *The*

Merry Drummer. Okudzhava's important novella *Lots of Luck, Kid!* is available in translation in *Pages from Tarusa* (Little, Brown, 1964) and, in an abridged version, in *Halfway to the Moon* (Holt, Rinehart & Winston, 1964).

Nikolai OSTROVSKY (1904–1936). Ostrovsky is the author of the "classic" Socialist Realist novel *How the Steel Was Tempered* (translated in English as *The Making of a Hero*) over 6,000,000 copies of which have been printed.

Boris PIL'NYAK (1891–1941?). Pil'nyak, whose real name was Vogau, was an important Russian modernist writer who was strongly influenced by Andrei Bely. He is best known for his novel *The Naked Year* written in 1922 (N.Y. 1928). In 1929 Pil'nyak published one of his works abroad, as a result of which he was expelled from the Writers' Union; he attempted to win back favor by writing a Five Year Plan novel, but failed. Pil'nyak was arrested and apparently shot in 1941, which is the date given in the latest Soviet scholarly reference to his death, although dates ranging from 1937 to 1940 have been given in the past. Pil'nyak stories are available in translation in the paperbacks *Great Soviet Short Stories* (Dell, 1962) and *Dissonant Voices in Soviet Literature* (Colophon, 1965).

Aleksei REMIZOV (1877–1957). Remizov, one of the most individualistic of modern Russian writers, was well-known long prior to 1917, and at his death in 1957 Remizov's novels, stories, and plays comprised a bulk comparable in scope to those of the major 19th century writers. Although many of his works have been translated into English, Remizov has never won his due recognition abroad, according to some, because he is the most "Russian" of modern Russian writers and therefore difficult for a foreigner to appreciate. Although he was an émigré, Remizov always remained withdrawn from politics (he much preferred the worlds of dreams and the ancient Russian past) as a result of which it is expected that he will become one of the Russian émigré writers to be "rehabilitated" in the Soviet Union. His best works available in English are *The Fifth Pestilence* (N.Y., 1928) and *The Clock* (London, 1924).

Konstantin PAUSTOVSKY (1893–   ). Paustovsky is one of the elder statesmen of Soviet letters, and his novels are read by millions in the Soviet Union. A "cautious liberal" throughout most of his life, Paustovsky has more and more in recent years been exerting himself in the cause of freedom of speech in the Soviet Union. His autobiography, *The Story of a Life* (Pantheon, 1964), received enthusiastic notices when it appeared in this country; also available in English are a series of essays on modern Russian writers in *Pages from Tarusa* (Little, Brown, 1964), a collection which was personally sponsored by Paustovsky.

Boris ROMASHOV (1895–1962). Romashov was the author of numerous Soviet propaganda plays in the 1940s.

Vasily ROZANOV (1856–1919). Rozanov was an outstanding Russian philosopher and critic. His thought, as set forth in such books as *Solitaria* (1912) and *Fallen Leaves*

(1913), attempts to cojoin sexuality and Christianity. As a critic Rozanov is best known for his brilliant study of Dostoevsky, *The Legend of the Grand Inquisitor* (1894). *Solitaria* (London, 1924) and *Fallen Leaves, Bundle One* (London, 1929) have been translated.

Robert ROZHDESTVENSKY (1932–   ). Rozhdestvensky is one of the poets of the "Evtushenko School." One of his political verses—an appeal for truthfulness—has been translated in the paperback *Year of Protest: 1956* (Vintage).

Lev SHESTOV (1866–1938). Shestov, whose real name was Shvartsman, has merit not only as an important Russian philosopher, but also—which is not too common among philosophers—as a master prose stylist. At the heart of Shestov's faith is a strong feeling of the irrationality of being, and so it is not surprising that he wrote extensively on Neitzsche, Dostoevsky, Kirkegaard, and Pascal. Among Shestov's books available in English are *All Things Are Possible* (in Russian, *The Apotheosis of Groundlessness;* NY, 1920) and *Anton Chekhov, and Other Essays* (London, 1916). Shestov emigrated from Russia in 1905.

Viktor SHKLOVSKY (1893–   ). Shklovsky, the most brilliant of the Russian Formalists (precursors of the American New Criticism), is today the outstanding living literary critic in the Soviet Union. In addition to his numerous books of literary criticism, Shklovsky is the author of a brilliant autobiography, written in the manner of Lawrence Sterne, *A Sentimental Journey* (1923). There is no English translation of this book (or any other of Shklovsky's books, for that matter), but a French transla-

tion *Voyage sentimental* (Paris, 1963) is available and highly recommended to those with a reading knowledge of French.

Ivan SHMELYOV (1873–1950). A Russian émigré writer of modest talent, Shmelyov is best known for *The Sun of the Dead* (1923), describing the horrors of the Civil War, which was translated into many languages. His other works include *The Man from a Restaurant, Soldiers, This Was,* and *The Inexhaustible Cup.*

Mikhail SHOLOKHOV (1905–   ). Sholokhov, a Cossack himself, is the best chronicler of that way of life in his stories *Tales of the Don* (Knopf, 1925) and his epic novel *The Quiet Don* (Knopf 1928–1940), one of the master-pieces of Soviet literature and one of the few novels which can bear comparison with *War and Peace*. In recent years, however, Sholokhov has written little; he is said to live in a baronial manner on his "estate" at Rostov-

on-the-Don, where he has a private airplane, servants, and even a theater troupe at his disposal, and spends much of his time hunting and drinking. Many Russian intellectuals are indignant at what they consider the squandering of a great talent.

Gustav SHPET (?). A prominent Russian philosopher of the 1920s whose works include *Aesthetic Fragments, The Philosophic Worldview of Herzen, Appearance and Meaning*, and *The Internal Form of the Word*.

Evgeny SHVARTS (1897–1958). In addition to numerous children's tales and two movie scenarios (one of which is *Don Quixote*), Shvarts is the author of eight superb and sophisticated adult fantasy-plays, the best of which are *The Naked King* (1934), *The Shadow* (1940), and *The Dragon* (1943). Many of Shvarts' plays could not be produced until 1960, and they are still staged infrequently although they enjoy immense popularity. Together with Mayakovsky and Babel, Shvarts seems assured of a place

as one of the very few Soviet dramatists of major stature. *The Shadow* has been translated in the paperback, *An Anthology of Russian Plays,* Vol. 2 (Vintage, 1963).

Konstantin SIMONOV (1915–   ). Simonov is a lyric poet and novelist. His best-known work, *Days and Nights* (1944), was the most popular Soviet World War II novel, but most of what he has since written has been disappointing if not cheap.

Ivan SOLONEVICH (1891–1953). Solonevich, a onetime Soviet concentration camp prisoner who escaped to the West, told his story in *Russia in a Concentration Camp* (1938) which was widely translated and read but, at the time, doubted.

Vladimir SOLOVYOV (1853–1900). Solovyov was one of the most important Russian religious philosophers and also a poet of note who strongly influenced many of the Russian Symbolists such as Blok and Bely. The best collection of Solovyov's writing in English is *A Solovyov Anthology* (Scribner's, 1950).

Aleksandr SOLZHENITSYN (1918–   ). Solzhenitsyn became known throughout the world with his first novella *One Day of Ivan Denisovich* (translated in English as *One Day in the Life of Ivan Denisovich*) which described life in a Soviet concentration camp. There are half a dozen translations of this work, but the Crest edition contains a rare interview with Solzhenitsyn and the Dutton edition contains the foreword by Aleksandr Tvardovsky which preceded *One Day* when it first appeared in *Novy Mir*. Solzhenitsyn has since written several other stories, and some very outspoken prose poems by him appeared in the West without having been printed in the Soviet Union in January, 1965 (*New Leader,* Jan. 18).

Viktor SOSNORA (?). Sosnora, who is held to be the foremost young poet of Leningrad, is the author of *January Cloudburst* (1962). Sosnora's poetry frequently employs motifs from medieval Russian tales and chronicles. One Sosnora poem has been translated into English in the anthology *Halfway to the Moon* (Holt, Rinehart & Winston; 1965).

Pyotr STRUVE (1870–1944). Struve was one of the foremost liberal thinkers of the Russian emigration. He wrote on the Russian Revolution, Lenin, and economic questions.

Aleksandr STEIN (1906–   ). A well-known Soviet dramatist who writes on topical questions.

Natalya TARASENKOVA (?). Tarasenkova is a young writer who, like her friend Yury Kazakov, cultivates the "Chekhovian manner" in her short stories. Her books include *Strange Dreams* and *How Can One Say All This*. Her best stories should be translated into English.

Aleksandr TAIROV (1885–1950). Tairov, a student of Meyerhol'd, founded the famous Kamerny Theatre in 1914. Tairov's dramatic method was non-realistic and utilized mimicry and gesticulation. After the Revolution Tairvo was frequently attacked in the Soviet press, and in 1939 he was relieved of his directorship and the Kamerny Theater was, in effect, abolished.

Vladimir TENDRYAKOV (1923–   ). One of the most pro-

lific young Soviet writers, Tendryakov's best novellas— the form he most favors—are *The Miraculous, Potholes, The Judgment,* and *Three, Seven, Ace.* The latter work has been translated in the collection *Dissonant Voices in Soviet Literature,* but the translation has been badly abridged and tampered with. *Potholes* has been translated in *Winter's Tales 7* (St. Martins, 1962).

Yury TRIFONOV (1925–   ). Trifonov is the author of the novel *Students.* One of his short stories, *Once on a Summer Night,* has been translated in *Pages from Tarusa* (Little, Brown, 1964).

Marina TSVETAEVA (1892–1941). Tsvetaeva's first poetry was published in 1911. Among her many books of poems are *Poems to Blok, Separation,* and *Craft.* After the 1917 Revolution, Tsvetaeva emigrated and lived for many years in Paris. In 1939, however, she returned to Russia, where, in 1941, she hanged herself under circumstances which have never been fully explained. Translations of five poems and a short story by Tsvetaeva are available in *Pages from Tarusa* (Little, Brown, 1964), and there are also three other poetic translations in *Tri-Quarterly* (Spring, 1965).

Vladimir TURBIN (?). Turbin is a young scholar whose book *Comrade Time, Comrade Art*—although less than 200 pages long—became something of a *cause célèbre* in the drive for literary freedom in the Soviet Union.

Aleksandr TVARDOVSKY (1910–   ). A much-respected Soviet poet, Tvardovsky's major works are *Vasily Tyorkin* (1946), a war poem whose hero is an unimportant comic soldier, and *Distance Beyond Distance* (1960 and *Tyorkin in the Other World* (1963), both of which have

played an important role in the campaign for de-Stalinization. Segments from *Vasily Tyorkin* appeared in *The
Atlantic* (June, 1960) and *Tyorkin in the Other World*
has been translated in its entirety in *Khrushchev and
the Arts* (M.I.T., 1965). Tvardovsky is editor of the
leading Soviet literary journal *Novy Mir*.

Aleksandr VERTINSKY (1889–1957). Vertinsky was a popular author and singer of exotic cabaret songs such as "The
Lilac-Colored Negro" and "The Tiny Little Creole." In
1945 he returned to the Soviet Union from emigration
and was greeted with much fanfare.

Evgeny VINOKUROV (1925–   ). Vinokurov is the author
of seven books of poetry, among them *The Word* (1962)
and *The Human Face* (1960). Several of the poems he
has written are among the best Russian poems of this
decade. There are translations of six Vinokurov poems in
Pages from Tarusa (Little, Brown, 1964).

Aleksandr VORONSKY (1884–1943). Voronsky was a leading Marxist critic who advocated a policy of permissive-
ness towards the arts. Voronsky himself wrote spirited
and keen essays on subjects as disparate as Marcel
Proust and proletarian literature. He had the distinction
of being arrested and sent to Siberia twice. The second
time he did not return.

Andrei VOZNESENSKY (1932–   ). Voznesensky's poems
began to appear in print in 1958. His first book of poetry,
Mozaika, appeared in 1960 in a provincial edition. His
subsequent books are *Parabola* and *40 Lyrical Digres-*

sions from the Triangular Pear, which is based in part on his trip to America in 1961. Voznesensky's ultra-modernistic long poem *Oza* has appeared in an English translation in *Tri-Quarterly* (Spring, 1965), and there are trans-

lations of his poems in *Halfway to the Moon* (Holt, Rinehart & Winston, 1965) and (with facing Russian texts) in *Odyssey* (December, 1962). Voznesensky is a poet of great promise.

Nikolai ZABOLOTSKY (1903–1958). Zabolotsky, although little known in the West, is, with Akhmatova and Pasternak, one of the great Russian poets of recent times. His poetic outlook is characterized by a curious and sly, but serious pan-animism which denies the possibility of death. Zabolotsky spent seven years in a Soviet concentration camp; he returned apparently unchanged, it is said, except that his family could not let him enter a store because he would try to buy everything "just in case." In addition to his own poetry, Zabolotsky learned

Georgian and translated almost the whole body of classical Georgian verse into lucid Russian poetry. Translations of four Zabolotsky poems are available in *Pages from Tarusa* (Little, Brown, 1964).

Boris ZAITSEV (1881–   ). Zaitsev, now the dean of Russian émigré writers, published his first book of stories in 1906. In addition to his novels and stories, Zaitsev has written biographies of Chekhov, Turgenev, and Zhukovsky.

Evgeny ZAMYATIN (1884–1937). One of the outstanding Russian modernists, Zamyatin is best known for his anti-utopian novel *We* (1924) which has been translated into many languages. Recently *We* was discussed, critically but at great length, in *Novy Mir*, indicating that there may be pressures to rehabilitate Zamyatin, who died an émigré in Paris as the result of a bold and unexpectedly successful request to Stalin himself to be allowed to leave Russia. One of Zamyatin's best short stories, *The Cave*, has been translated in *Great Soviet Short Stories* (Dell, 1962).

D. ZATONSKY (?). Zatonsky is a Soviet scholar specializing in Western European literature. Among his books are *The 20th Century—Notes on Literary Form in the West* and *Hero and Author—The fate of Realism in the Contemporary Foreign Novel*.

Vasily ZENKOVSKY (1881–1962). Zenkovsky is the author of the standard history of Russian philosophy, *A History of Russian Philosophy,* which is available in English (Columbia, 1953).

Andrei ZHDANOV (1895–1948). "Cultural" commissar under Stalin.

Tamara ZHIRMUNSKAYA (1936–   ). Zhirmunskaya's poetic voice concentrates on "the earthly madonnas" and "the generation that came down from the mountains." She has written many fine poems, none of which have been translated.

Mikhail ZOSHCHENKO (1895–1958). Zoshchenko was the great modern Soviet humorist who perfectly captured the spirit of his time. There has been a recent translation of his stories, *Nervous People* (Pantheon, 1963). He was expelled from the Writers' Union in 1946.

MIHAJLOV'S OPEN LETTER TO RISTO TOSOVIC, EDITOR OF *NIN*

Dear Sir, Editor in Chief of *Nin:*

I reserve the right to call you "Sir," since you addressed me as such in your editorial yesterday.

Of course, I do not expect you to publish this letter. You probably recall that six weeks ago I sent you another letter, protesting the removal of the so-called "chief" editor of the journal *Kolo,* Sasha Veres, for publishing my article "Dostoevsky Today" in the sixth and seventh issues of his journal.

In that article I "ventured" to express the heretical view that even Christianity, as a religion of freedom, can become the basis for a just organization of society on earth, and not the so-called "natural laws of development," on which the theory of "scientific" socialism is based; that a belief in the immortality of the individual human soul by no means excludes, but on the contrary justifies, the struggle for the "kingdom of liberty" on earth; and, specifically, that reason alone, unaccompanied by belief in immortality, negates this struggle.

I protested against the gross administrative obstacles to the printing of the third section of my article, in which I expressed this thought—after having criticized, in the

209

first two parts of the article, the idea of progress as a scientific-technical forward movement.

Naturally, when referring to "Christianity" I had no particular church in mind.

You will remember that I warned you: If your paper refused (like *Telegram* and *Vjesnik*) to take up this obvious case of a relic of *Zhdanovshchina* in our country, I would consider it not only my duty but my obligation to inform the foreign press about everything that has occurred, and to provide all documentary evidence.

Despite your refusal to publish the letter, I did not do this. Perhaps that was a mistake. But I still believe that, of all the socialist countries, Yugoslavia is the most democratic; I held back because of the possibility that I might bring harm to Yugoslavia's reputation in the world.

However, after your editorial yesterday entitled "Mihajlo Mihajlov's Strange Summer," I cannot and do not wish to remain silent.

Dear Mr. Editor-in-Chief! Your editorial staff called me a "White Russian," "interventionist," "Mister," and "Right-wing agent of White Russian and anti-Communist circles."

Mr. Editor-in-Chief of *Nin:* When World War II began in Europe I was five years old. When the Civil War and the intervention ended in Russia, and when my parents arrived in Yugoslavia, my father was 17 years of age and my mother seven. My father studied and graduated at a *Yugoslav* university, did his military service in the *Yugoslav* Army, took an active part in the *Yugoslav* national liberation struggle, and for years directed the *Yugoslav* Scientific Institute.

I was born in the *Yugoslav* town of Pancevo, attended primary school in the *Yugoslav* town of Zrenjanin, completed my secondary education in the *Yugoslav* town of Sarajevo, attended and graduated from universities in the *Yugoslav* cities of Belgrade and Zagreb, constructed a *Yugoslav* highway in the ranks of the youth work brigades, served a term in the *Yugoslav* Army, was elected instructor at a *Yugoslav* university, and in my documents, under the heading "Nationality," the word "Yugoslav" is written.

Mr. Tosovic, I despise you! Not for myself, but for my friends and readers throughout Yugoslavia, am I compelled to answer all the lies, all the distortions about my travel notes contained in your editorial.

You are probably well aware that I was not in the Soviet Union as a "tourist," as you repeatedly state. I spent a whole month in the USSR in 1964 under the Cultural Exchange Program of the USSR and the Socialist Federal Republic of Yugoslavia. A Soviet university instructor made a return visit of one month to Yugoslavia. I was no one's "guest," and had no need to lie about what I saw in gratitude for the hospitality shown me!

What can one do? I feel more respect for the Russian people than for the Soviet authorities. I did not abuse anybody's confidence. I did not write a single word about my conversations with distinguished Russian authors without receiving their permission for this in advance whenever it was a case of conversations without witnesses. And do not suppose that I was able to write about everything which I discussed and which I came to know.

Unfortunately your editorial, in its parts and as a whole, gives the opposite meaning of everything I wrote, and unjustly leaves me in an unequal position.

A "temporary ban" is in effect on the second number of the journal *Delo*, and publication of the third part of my travel notes—in which I set out the main conclusions of my stay in Moscow—is not even planned.

Only one possibility remains for me: to appeal to my friends and readers throughout the country to compare the assertions made in your editorial with the first, unprohibited part of my travel notes, and with my article "Dostoevsky's *House of the Dead* and Solzhenitsyn," in the Journal of the Yugoslav Academy of Sciences and Art, *Forum*, No. 6, 1964, in which I clearly defined my outlook regarding Stalinism and socialism.

Your editorial is couched in the style of the coarsest "practice of ideological justice" from the time of A. A. Zhdanov and is aimed at intimidating *not only, and not so much myself* but all those who have any kind of "original" ideas.

I did not reveal any particularly new facts about the USSR. Six or seven years ago, articles were appearing in this country which described all these things openly, and more harshly. Just think of the book by Margaret Buber-Neumann, *Under Two Dictators*, Weissberg's *Conspiracy of Silence*, Gregory Klimov's *The Terror Machine*, and so on.

That is to say, there is no question here of the facts

which I mentioned, but rather of the fact that I mentioned them in an "original" (your term) fashion. In other words, it is a question of my daring, without permission, to think with my own head and look around with my own eyes.

This is a question of the fact that, in a country where serfdom still prevails (since the agricultural workers are administratively bound to the *kolkhoz*), I devoted more attention in an "original" way to the songs which ordinary Russians sing than to the flashy publicity about space rockets.

You ask, in a threatening tone: "What are the new 'ideas' Mihajlo Mihajlov is thinking about?" Esteemed Mr. Editor: Thanks to the fact that, fortunately, Yugoslavia is not the USSR, I have for years been publicly and openly voicing my ideas in my numerous articles and essays in Yugoslav newspapers and journals (*Telegram, Vjesnik, Nase Teme, Danas, Kolo, Kritika, Forum, Letopis Matica Srpska, Delo, 15 Days, Razlog*), in broadcasts on the Yugoslav radio, and at open lectures before the most varied audiences in Zagreb and Zadar.

I am prepared at any time, if you will grant me space in your newspaper, to explain and document all my attitudes and assertions, from statistical data on the rapid increase in alcoholism and hooliganism in the USSR to the "mysticism from the arsenal of the Middle Ages," as my philosophy is described by the critic Miodrag Bogicevic in the February 11, 1965 issue of *Komunist*.

I should like to mention that one of the people who thinks like me is a well-known obscurantist of our century, who wrote the following words: "The most beautiful excitement which we can experience is mystical. This is the progenitor of all real art and science. The man to whom this excitement is foreign is no longer able to experience wonder, or to stand bewildered and in fearful admiration, just as if he were dead."

And his name is—Albert Einstein.

And another important contemporary *Marxist* figure, Lucien Goldmann, has written this: "We are . . . completely in agreement with the idea . . . that modern socialist thought has been able to thrive only within the intellectual and affective world which Christian thought and culture created." (L. Goldmann, *Dialectical Materialism,* p. 92, Sarajevo, 1962.)

Mr. Editor, I do not hide the fact that I consider Vladimir Solovyov, Emmanuel Mounier, Teilhard de Chardin, Aurobindo, Shestov and Berdyaev to be greater, more profound thinkers than any living Marxist philosopher. I do not conceal the fact that I consider myself a Christian.

Your paper does not scare me by accusing me of "anti-Communism." Believe me, I am not the only one who feels that it was one and the same hand that killed Garcia Lorca and Maxim Gorky, Dimitrije Tucevic and Tukhachevsky, Patrice Lumumba and Imre Nagy. I am deeply convinced that every increase in the strength of Stalinism at the same time signifies and assists the growth of neo-Nazism; and if your attitude were to gain the upper hand in Yugoslavia—however paradoxical this may seem—this would entail the strengthening of McCarthyism, even over there in the U.S.A.

I will take legal action against your newspaper for defamation and malicious and deliberate deception of our public.

Since I am sure you will not publish this letter, I am sending copies of it to the editorial boards of all Yugoslav newspapers.

[Signed] MIHAJLO MIHAJLOV

> *University Lecturer in the town of Zadar, a town which the latest edition of the Great Soviet Encyclopedia describes as "an American military base on the Mediterranean."*

[March 1, 1965]

INDEX

Akhmadulina, Bella, 32, 33, 85–88, 174–175, 176
Akhmatova, Anna, 25, 62, 86, 175, 206
Alyoshin, Samuil, 54–56, 175
Anders, Günter, 21
Andreev, Leonid, 37, 175–176
Andrić, Ivo, 17
Antokol'sky, Pavel, 87, 176
Artistic Prose, 98, 100
Asimov, Isaac, 30

Babel, Isaac, 24, 176, 201
Babovic, Milislav, 17
Bakhtin, M. M., 17, 26–27, 30
Balakin, M. S., 17
Beckett, Samuel, 22
Bedny, Demyan, 176
Belinsky, Vissarion, 99, 176–177
Bely, Andrei, 19, 35, 37, 87, 122, 177
Berdyaev, Nikolai, 103–104, 131, 139–140, 166, 167, 177–178, 214
Bloch, Ernst, 23, 178
Brod, Max, 21
Bondaryov, Yury, 88–93, 178
Brecht, Bertolt, 30
Bugaev, see Bely, Andrei
Bukharin, Nikolai, 17, 178
Bulgahov, Sergei, 178

Camus, Albert, 22
Chalmaev, V., 32

Chernyshevsky, Nikolai, 178
Chirkov, 26
Chukovsky, Kornei, 24fn
Chukovsky, Nikolai, 24, 179
Comrade Time, Comrade Art, 114–115
Ćopić, Branko, 17
Cosić, Dobrica, 17
Couple, The, 89–90

Danilevsky, Nikolai, 179
Dead Men's Sun, 70
de Chardin, Teilhard, 103, 214
Dik, Iosif, 33
Djordjevic-Grigorijev, Radmila, 17
Dostoevsky, Fyodor, 16–17, 26–27, 30, 91–92, 104, 161
Dostoevsky and Kant, 38, 40, 183
Dr. Zhivago, 20, 47
Dudintsev, Vladimir, 20, 30, 33, 41–47, 53, 179–180
Dymshits, 27

Ehrenburg, Ilya, 24fn, 46, 119–126, 167, 180–181
Eliot, T. S., 22, 130
Ermilov, Vladimir, 27, 181
Ern, Vladimir, 181
Esenin, Sergei, 181
Esenina, Tatyana, 182
Esenin-Volpin, Aleksandr, 181–182

217

Evtushenko, Evgeny, 32, 33, 131, 158, 174, 182

Fadeev, Aleksandr, 182
Florovsky, Georges, 182
Foundling, 95
Frank, Simon, 182–183
Freud, Sigmund, 23
Friedlander, G. M., 27,
Fromm, Erich, 23, 151–152
Fyodorov, Nikolai, 102–103, 183

Glazunov, Ilya, 14, 183
Goldmann, Lucien, 23, 183, 214
Golosovker, Yakov E., 38–41, 183
Golosovsky, Igor, 54, 184
Gonchar, Oles, 23, 184
Gorbatov, A. V., 66–68, 184
Gorky, Maxim, 25–26, 32, 184, 214
Granin, Daniil, 53, 184–185
Grigorev, Apollon, 185
Grin, Aleksandr, 27–29, 185
Grinevsky, see Grin, Aleksandr
Gudzy, Nikolai, 35–36, 185
Gumilyov, Nikolai, 24–26, 185–186
Gus, Mikhail S., 102, 103, 186

Hamlet (film), 50–51
Heidegger, Martin, 23
Hemingway, Ernest, 22, 100
Herzen, Aleksandr, 186
Hospital Ward, The (play), 54–56, 175

Ilichyov, Leonid, 33, 95, 108, 115, 136, 187
Il'in, Ivan, 187
I Want to Believe (play), 54

James, Henry, 22
Jaspers, Karl, 23
Joyce, James, 22, 23, 30, 88, 100
Julio Jurenito 120–121, 126, 167–168, 181

Kafka, Franz, 19, 20–22, 103
Kazakov, Yury, 33, 187
Kazakova, Rimma, 33, 187
Khlebnikov, Velemir, 87, 188
Kichko, Trofin, 140–141
Klomov, Georgy, 142
Kochetov, Vsevolod, 45, 188
Kol'man, E., 151
Kodryanskaya, Natalya, 36
Krapchenko, 27
Krleza, 17,

Lakshin, V. I., 126
Lamumba, Patrice, 82–83, 214
Lawrence, D. H., 22
Lavrenyov, Boris, 61, 188
Leonov, Leonid, 27, 46, 62–66, 188–189
Leont'ev, Konstantin, 104, 124, 137–138, 189
Lie for a Narrow Circle, A (play), 54
Lipatov, Vik, 33, 42, 189
Lorca, Garcia, 214
Lossky, Nikolai, 104, 138, 189
Lots of Luck, Kid!, 109
Lukacs, Georg, 23, 169, 189–190
Lunacharksky, Anatoly, 40, 190
Luxemburg, Rosa, 168

Maksimović, Desanka, 17
Malevich, Kasimir, 19, 190
Mandelstam, Osip, 24, 86, 190
Mann, Thomas, 22, 70
Marshak, Samuil, 191

Martynov, Leonid, 33, 129, 132, 191

Matveeva, Novella, 33, 46, 47, 133, 191

Maugham, Somerset, 22

Mayakovsky, Vladimir, 87, 99, 114, 115, 130, 131, 192–193, 201

Merezhkovsky, Dmitri, 193

Meyerhol'd, Vsevolod, 56, 193

Mikhailovsky, Boris, 36–38, 193

Mochul'sky, Konstantin, 91–92, 194

Mounier, Emmanuel, 23, 194, 214

Morits, Yuna, 33, 194

Music, 117

Myasnikov, 27

Nabokov, Vladimir, 19

Nagibin, Yury, 174, 194

Naked King, The (play), 61

Nekrasov, Viktor, 194–195

New Year's Tale, A, 179–180

Nikitin, Sergei, 33, 195

Nilin, Pavel, 33, 195

Not By Bread Alone, 41, 47, 179

Okudzhava, Bulat, 33, 76, 87, 104–114, 195–196

One Day in the Life of Ivan Denisovich, 127, 128

Ostrovsky, Nikolai, 161, 196

Ozerov, Valery, 32, 47, 94

Pages from Tarusa, 33–34, 197

Pasternak, Boris, 17, 20, 47, 86, 87, 101, 130–131, 152, 159, 163, 206

Paustovsky, Konstantin, 24fn, 29, 33, 48, 89, 197

Pertsov, 27

Pil'nyak, Boris, 17, 196

Pilyar, Evgeny, 71

Pridvorov, see Bedney, Demyan

Proust, Marcel, 22, 30, 87–88

Quiet Flows the Don, 100

Remizov, Aleksei, 35–36, 37, 65, 103, 196–197

Romashov, Boris, 58, 197

Rozanov, Vasily, 104, 198–199

Roshdestvensky, Robert, 33, 149, 198

Salinsky, Afanasy, 54

Sarukhanova, Svetlana, 27

Shadow, The (play), 57–61

Shchipachyov, Stephan, 130

Shestov, Lev, 17, 104, 122, 150, 198, 214

Shklovsky, Viktor, 27, 98–104, 138, 177, 198–199

Shmelyov, Ivan, 70, 199

Sholokhov, Mikhail, 27, 31, 74, 75, 100, 199–200

Shpet, Gustov, 200

Shvarts, Evgeny, 57–62, 200–201

Shvartsman, see Shestov, Lev

Silence, 88–89, 178

Simonov, Konstantin, 71–74, 201

Soldiers Are Not Born, 71–74

Solonevich, Ivan, 68, 201

Solovyov, Vladimir, 15, 104, 138, 139–140, 152, 201–202, 214

Solzhenitsyn, Aleksandr, 23, 33, 66, 127, 128, 202

Sosnora, Viktor, 33, 202

Stein, Aleksandr, 61, 62, 203

Struve, Pyotr, 202

Tairov, Aleksandr, 56, 203
Tarasenkova, Natalya, 33, 203
Tendryakov, Vladimir, 33, 93–
97, 203–204
Thief, The, 63, 64
Three, Seven, Ace, 93, 94
Tight Knot, A, 94
Tolstoy, Leo, 99–100, 102, 103,
125, 150
Trifonov, Yury, 204
Tsudnelovich, 26
Tsvetaeva, Marina, 33, 86, 204
Turbin, Vladimir N., 30, 114–
116, 204
Tvardovsky, Alexsandr, 127–
128, 204–205

Unknown Soldier, The, 44, 45

Vasylevskaya, 27
Vazhdaev, V., 29
Vertinsky, Aleksandr, 51, 61,
205

Vinokurov, Evgeny, 33, 116–
119, 192, 205
Voronsky, Aleksandr, 31, 205
Voznesensky, Andrei, 32, 33,
86, 129–133, 205–206

Walk Toward the Storm,
(play), 53
White Flag, The, 95
Woolf, Virginia, 22, 88

Zabolotsky, Nikolai, 33, 206–
207
Zaitsev, Boris, 24, 207
Zamyatin, Evgeny, 17, 25, 34,
35, 65, 116, 207
Zatonsky, D., 20–22, 207
Zenkovsky, Vasily, 207–208
Zestev, M., 74
Zhdanov, Andrei, 62, 208, 212
Zhirmunskaya, Tamara, 33, 47–
49, 208
Zoshchenko, Mikhail, 62, 208

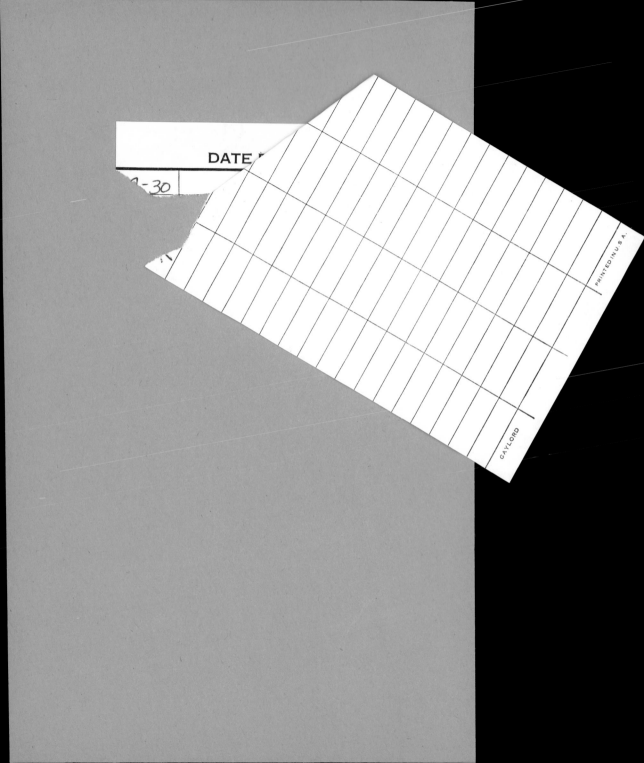

DATE

-30

GAYLORD   PRINTED IN U.S.A.